VICTORIAN HIGH-WHEELERS

— the early social life of the bicycle where Dorset meets Hampshire

Roger T. C. Street

DORSET PUBLISHING CO
KNOCK-NA-CRE   MILBORNE PORT
SHERBORNE   DORSET DT9 5HJ

Contents

Preface	3
Wheels start turning	4
Runs and races	11
Fireworks and functions	17
Local meets	21
Declining years	29
Metamorphosis	35
Clarke the cycle seller	38
Persecution and prosecution	42
Mudeford Bicycle Club	45
The Dual Tricycle	48
Calendar of events	50
Recorded members	53
Club songs	55
Text references	57
Index	59

Dedicated to the CRABS, the members of the Christchurch Ramshackle Antique Bicycle Society, who are today's true heirs to the Victorian tradition.

First published 1979 by Dorset Publishing Company, Knock-na-cre, Milborne Port, Sherborne, Dorset DT9 5HJ. Copyright © Roger T. C. Street, 1979.
No part of this publication may be reproduced, stored in a retrieval system, or transmitted in any form or by any means, electronic, mechanical, photocopying, recording or otherwise, without prior permission.
Printed by Cox, Sons and Co Limited of Williton, Somerset.
ISBN 0 902129 31 7.

Preface

TRANSPORT HISTORY is in vogue. Railway books are legion. Yet the number of works on the early years of the bicycle—an invention still much employed throughout the world—are comparatively few. Such modern works as are available tend to be general histories of the development of the machine from the hobby-horse onwards. In this book the author hopes to start to redress the balance by providing a close view of a particular cycling organisation active for a short while at the beginning of the era (if we discount the early ventures) about a hundred years ago. Those masters of the 'high' or 'ordinary' bicycle (later called the 'penny-farthing') were the members of the Christchurch Bicycle Club, which was in existence from 1876 to 1884 on the borders of Hampshire and Dorset.

Although this is primarily a history of one individual early bicycle club, it also serves as a good example of the picture generally at this date. The sort of cycling and other activities indulged in by the Christchurch Bicycle Club were undertaken by many similar societies up and down the country, as the cycling literature of the period clearly shows. The Christchurch club was but a star in this firmament.

The basic pattern of the work is a chronological account through six chapters of the history of the club and its activities, followed by four chapters on related local topics. Appendices provide a calendar of events, analysis of recorded membership and collection of club songs.

Most of the material for this book has come from local newspapers (principally the *Christchurch Times* and *Bournemouth Observer and Christchurch Chronicle*) and national cycling periodicals (principally *Bicycling News*, *The Bicycling Times*, *Cycling*, *The Cyclist* and *Wheel World*). It was too much to hope that the club records—like minute book and rules—would still be extant, though unsuccessful efforts to locate them were made. However the press coverage is so good, partly due to an indefatigable club secretary, that the gap is much less significant than it would otherwise be.

I acknowledge the friendly help of the staff at the headquarters of the Cyclists Touring Club in Godalming, the British Library at Colindale, the Red House Museum in Christchurch and the Bournemouth Reference Library, where much of the research work has taken place. Above all I am deeply grateful to Christchurch local historian Allen White, whose photographs of the club set me on the trail and who has supplied a number of the illustrations as well as considerable advice and moral support.

1. Wheels start turning

To see a dozen or a score of men astride their silent horses, uniformly dressed, each rider in his place, and all regulating their speed by the captain, as they glide smoothly and swiftly along a country lane is a sight fascinating to a stranger and gratifying to a brother bicyclist. They tower above the hedge, and often you can see them following the winding road by the hill side, now disappearing in a hollow, now mounting a slight rise; when the hedge is low you can see their legs moving, and in the bright sunshine the polished ironwork glistens as the wheels revolve. To a non-rider how easy must the motion seem, how soft and quiet the movement.[1]

ERNEST CLARKE started it all.   He had come from Coventry, where the bicycle industry had flourished since the beginning of the decade. He opened his cycle business in Christchurch in 1873.   No doubt he had thoughts of increasing his turnover.   But just as surely he was fired with a non-financial enthusiasm for his new project—the formation in 1876 of the Christchurch Bicycle Club.

Strangely, none of the local newspapers or national cycling periodicals seem to have noticed the inauguration, even though it was the first club of its kind in the area.   Our information has therefore to be extracted from reports of speeches made after the club's existence had been recognised by the press.   One of the early members, James Lawrence, tells us that Mr. Clarke "had been captain since the club was started, the captain and himself having been the first bicyclists in the town".[2]   Edward Ernest himself adds that the club "started in July, 1876, with four members.   On July 12 of the same year the first run was made to Sopley, when five started, and that was considered a good number."[3] According to the *Bicycle Annual* of 1878, the actual date of formation was Thursday 6 July 1876.

Bicycle clubs had been growing in number since 1869 (when the Aston Star Club was established in Birmingham).   The *Wheelman's Year Book* for 1882 reveals there were less than twenty-five provincial clubs at the beginning of 1874, less than fifty at the beginning of 1875, less than seventy-five at the beginning of 1876—but more than one hundred and fifty by the beginning of 1877 and over six hundred by 1880.   So 1876 can be regarded as the 'take-off' year.

This is supported by an editorial in the *Bicycle Journal* for 20 October 1876, which announces: "There has been a wonderful increase of bicycle clubs, which are now more than double the number in existence at the beginning of the year".

The Christchurch club was a fruit of this harvest.   Referring to the proposed formation of a club at Poole the following year, the local paper says: "Bicycle clubs are now established in most of the large towns throughout the country, their object is to train members in the art of bicycle riding, to see that offences against the public are not wantonly committed by careless and indiscreet riding, and also to protect the members from the stupid treatment they sometimes receive from pedestrians, drivers and others, by whom their lives are occasionally imperilled." [4]

The first fully reported run took place on 31 May 1877. No doubt there were others following the short opening excursion to Sopley but they are not recorded. Certainly by the late spring of the following year the club had acquired a number of new members and was prepared to tackle a lengthy expedition:

The Christchurch Bicycle Club met early on Monday morning at the top of High Street for a run out. Ten of the members and a friend or two started at about 8.15 for Salisbury, their numbers being supplemented to seventeen by the time they reached Burton. A splendid run was made after stopping at Fordingbridge and Downton for refreshments. The party reached Salisbury about 12 without any very serious mishap. One or two of the riders came to the ground,, without doing any great damage to their machines or injury to themselves. After a short stay in Salisbury the party returned, reaching home a little before 7.

A little amusement was indulged in when coming home. At Sopley several members of the Yeomanry were on the road and attempted to overtake the bicyclists, but failed to do so, the riders of the wheeled machines being a little too good for them. The club took the lead at starting and retained it till they arrived at Christchurch.

Mr. E. Clarke, the captain, and Mr. W. E. Burt, sub-captain of the club, accompanied the party. [5]

This is an interesting report for a number of reasons. It suggests there were already more than fifteen members of the club, under the captaincy of Ernest Clarke. The complete trip would have been over fifty miles, the route being in fact described in the "tourist's guide" section of *Bicycling: its Rise and Development* in 1874: "Salisbury to Christchurch, via Fordingbridge, 26 miles. The road is nearly all gravel, and after the first three miles almost a dead level, with a good surface, but in portions inclined to be sandy." The reference "one or two riders came to the ground" is not an uncommon one. The general condition of the roads at this time left much to be desired, and a large stone or pot-hole could easily give rise to a 'cropper', usually—but not always—without serious harm resulting. The 'Yeomanry' were the Bournemouth Yeomanry Cavalry. It is perhaps surprising to learn that the new 'iron horses' could outpace the older variety over a distance of about three miles.

The next recorded event is less fully reported:

Bicycle Club. On Thursday evening, nine members of this club and a few friends had a fine run to Lymington, starting from Purewell at about six and arriving at their destination shortly after seven. After strolling round the town for about an hour they started on the return journey, arriving home about nine. Mr. E. Clarke, captain of the club, was present, Mr. Walter Jenkins acting as sub-captain. [6]

This was a total distance of about twenty-two miles, covered in about two hours, at the very fair speed of eleven miles an hour each way. Briefer, though, was the coverage for a bicycle race which "took place on Friday week between Mr. Fred Phillips of Thorney hill and Mr. James Frampton of Newtown" (now Highcliffe) "starting from the Cat & Fiddle Inn to Bransgore recreation ground, which terminated in favour of Mr. Phillips." [7] Mr. Frampton was a member of the Christchurch club.

The only other ordinary run reported for 1877 is one to Bournemouth (about six miles each way) in the autumn:

Christchurch Bicycle Club. On Thursday evening, September 27th, a capital meet of this club took place in the High Street. The party numbering fourteen started about 6 p.m. for Bournemouth, through Pokesdown and Boscombe to the Lansdowne Hotel, where a turn was made to the right and a run made up the Holdenhurst road, to opposite the Heathpoult. The party then turned and ran back the same road to the Square, via the old Christchurch road, where a dismount was made and the bicycles stacked. The start home was made by way of the Bath Hotel, and Christchurch reached about 7.30 p.m., all being well pleased with their ride. Thursday being the last early closing evening of the shops, most of the members of the club availed themselves of the opportunity of a meet, and this may be considered the most successful of the season; Mr. E. Clarke, captain of the club, took command of the party, and Mr. C. W. Bollard acted as sub-captain. [8]

The Landsdowne Hotel and the Bath Hotel still flourish, but the 'Heathpoult' has long since gone. It was in fact an inn on the corner of Heathpoult Road (now St. Paul's Road) and Holdenhurst Road, an 1873 estate map at the local Springbourne library shows. The reference to "Thursday being the last early closing evening of the shops" is somewhat revealing. A number of the members of the club were local shopkeepers, or sons of shopkeepers, who would find difficulty in attending during opening hours.

Again we are fortunate to have a contemporaneous description of a route taken by the Christchurch riders, as recorded by a tourist in the area:

The journey begins with a short climb up the Bath Hotel hill, at Bournemouth, and this done, the rider has a short run over a shaky road in most parts loose as far as Christchurch (5 miles), one hill, and that a short one, is encountered at Boscombe (1 mile); the rest is level with the exception of a descent at Pokesdown, which demands considerable care, as it is generally stony.[9]

The last event of the year took place on Boxing Day, and was an unusual one:

On Wednesday a paper chase was held by the C.B.C. who assembled at the meet in the High Street, at 10.15. Messrs. Jenkins and Frampton were appointed hares, and the hounds were in charge of the captain and sub-captain (Messrs. E. Clarke and W. Street), a start of three minutes was given, and after a run of about 25 miles a capital finish was made, the hares running home with about 300 yards to spare, the first hounds to arrive were Messrs. Clarke, Street and Gosling.[10]

The *Bournemouth Observer* adds that ten members assembled for this "splendid run." Although neither newspaper refers expressly to the use of bicycles, these would of course have been employed, and indeed bicycle paper chases were an occasional diversion of various clubs at this period. Jenkins and Frampton were two of the club's fastest racers, as we shall see later.

How was the club managed during this initial period? In the absence of club records we cannot be categoric, but it would seem that to start with there had been a fairly simple set of rules, containing no provision for a committee. The day-to-day management was probably left to the secretary, the energetic and hard-working C. W. Bollard, and runs were under the control of the captain and sub-captain (who would be at the front and rear respectively). The election of new members was dealt with in general meeting. After fifteen months the club had a membership of about twenty and a more sophisticated arrangement was thought desirable.

So a new code of rules was drawn up containing a provision for a committee in addition to the existing officers, and four members were duly elected. The annual subscription of the club was fixed at ten shillings, and the entrance fee at two shillings and sixpence. The opportunity was also taken to lay down some rules of the road, including provisions that "members of the club are not allowed to practise in the street", "members are particularly requested to have a bell attached to their machines" and "members shall ride in single file." All this can be gathered from the reports of three general meetings at the Temperance Hotel in September and October, 1877,[11] and subsequent items in the local newspaper.[12]

It was at the third of the general meetings, on 15 October (when the new rules were finally adopted), that the club decided to make the Temperance Hotel in Castle Street, Christchurch, their headquarters and club-room. So far as we know, there had previously been no such facility provided. This arrangement did not last for long, however. In January, 1878, we learn that "Christchurch Bicycle Club have now taken a room in Mr. Rose's house in the High Street, which is used as a reading room by the members".[13] Mr. James Rose and his son Henry both lived and worked in the High Street as cabinet makers and upholsterers.[14] This was "a nice club-room," with papers supplied for the use of the members,[15] and presumably offered greater privacy than the hotel accommodation.

Despite the club-room comforts, the members kept riding through the winter months. There were at least three local runs during January 1878, and on the last day of the month there was a strong turn-out to see the Prince of Wales at Crichel House (north of Wimborne) where he was staying as the guest of Lord Alington. The *Bournemouth Observer* reported:

Bicycle Club. On Thursday about nineteen members of the Christchurch Bicycle Club assembled in the High-street and proceeded to Crichel to see the meet, (a report of which will be found elsewhere) the roads were in capital condition for bicycling and a splendid run was made to Wimborne where, after a short stay, the party proceeded on their way, the road from Wimborne to Crichel being lined with horses and conveyances of every kind. After several dismounts the park was reached about 11.15 and the party proceeded to near Crichel House where they were rewarded with a fine view of the meet. The return journey commenced about 2.30 and arriving at Wimborne, the bicyclists dismounted and partook of dinner at the Crown after which the party started for Christchurch which was reached about 6 p.m. All were delighted with the day's outing. In the absence of Mr. Clarke, Mr. W. Street (sub-captain) acted as captain and Mr. C. W. Bollard, as sub-captain. One or two of the younger members of the Club though plucky in attempting such a long journey, gave up on the return journey to Wimborne, and came home by rail.[16]

The total journey was in fact about 34 miles. Another report on the same page provides some colourful details of the main event. This was a lawn meet of the East Dorset Hunt in front of Lord Alington's residence. It was calculated that 12,000 people were present. The Prince and Princess appeared on the East balcony and were "enthusiastically cheered", after which the hounds were brought on to the lawn by the "noble master", the Royal party and the ladies and gentlemen present then proceeding through the park on the road to Long Crichel.

The reference in the Bicycle Club report to the fact that "one or two of the younger members . . . came home by rail" reminds us that although bicycles were the earliest mechanical road users, the

ENVIRONS OF CHRISTCHURCH.

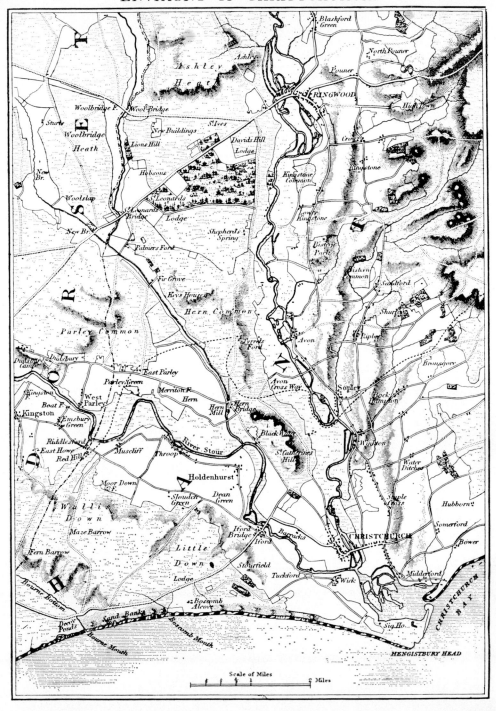

Scale of Miles

Miles

HENGISTBURY HEAD

CHRISTCHURCH BAY

Christchurch Bicycle Club in 1879. The top picture shows W. A. Marshall (left) with what appears to be a quadricycle. It has a large seat instead of a saddle. Others in the picture, to his right, are G. Gossling, J. Lawrence, C. Payn and F. Bemister. *Below:* prominent in the foreground are C. W. Bollard, the club secretary, and (with bugle) Ernest Clarke. In the background, left to right, are J. Lawrence, C. Payn, F. Bemister, W. C. Sparkes, J. Frampton and A. J. Salter.

railway system was already well-established by the advent of the high-wheelers. It provided a useful means of transporting bicyclist and machine to distant parts of the realm to take part in meets or races, could be employed during tours (as we shall see) and when necessary even on local runs, for example, in case of accident or fatigue. During the years the club was active the main line ran from Brockenhurst to Ringwood, then on to Wimborne, Poole and Bournemouth West. There was a branch line from Ringwood to Christchurch (with a stop at Hurn), and on to Bournemouth. The line from Christchurch to Brockenhurst came a little later, as also did the link between the two Bournemouth stations.

The last run of the 1877–78 season was to Ringwood on Monday 18 March, a total distance of some eighteen miles. At the annual dinner the following day, Clarke observed that the return journey (nine miles) was made in 41 minutes, "and this was fair travelling, considering there was a young member amongst them". An average speed of about $13\frac{1}{2}$ miles an hour, certainly not bad on the roads of the time.

The club's first annual dinner was fully reported in both the local and the cycling press. It seems there were some twenty-five to thirty members and friends present. Captain Clarke was in the chair. The venue was The Ship in the High Street, at that stage a hotel (later to be nominated for members' use by the Bicycle Touring Club). We are told that "a capital repast was provided by host Matthews, to which ample justice was done". Then followed a large number of toasts and speeches, including naturally "The Christchurch Bicycle Club". The Captain, in responding to a toast to his health, referred to the fact that "the club had not gone back since its commencement, and of the thirty who had been enrolled, only six had since left, three of whom had left the town and one had given up riding." He said the seasons runs had totalled "altogether about 280 miles, which was not much". The recorded runs for the year to March, 1878, total at a rough estimate about two-thirds of this figure at most. There are probably about another half-dozen to a dozen rides to be accounted for. The club was getting into its stride.

Another matter referred to by Captain Clarke was the nomination of Sir Henry Drummond Woolf MP as president of the club. This had in fact taken place at the general meeting the previous October, when a letter of acceptance had been read out and "acknowledged with great applause". Sir Henry was the local Conservative member of Parliament from 1874 to 1880, when he retired and the seat was won by the Liberal candidate Horace Davey Q.C. The new member accepted a vice-presidential post, but Sir Henry stayed on as president. There is no evidence that he took a particularly active interest in the affairs of the club (he was unable to attend any of the reported annual dinners), and it seems fair to regard him primarily as a figurehead.

A feature of the 1878 and subsequent dinners, and indeed of club events generally, was the singing of songs. Whilst this was a general pursuit in Victorian times, it deserves special mention in connection with Christchurch Bicycle Club, if only because the club had amongst its members quite an accomplished composer. J. W. White's song *Bicycle Riding* (reproduced facing pages 52 & 53)was written expressly for the dinner, was subsequently published and acquired national fame. We read for example that "the new cycling song *Bicycle Riding* went off immensely at the annual dinner of the Newcastle A.B.C.".[17] A review states "the phraseology is pretty good, the rhyme is passable, and both music and words are easy to learn and remember"[18]—but the reader can judge for himself by turning to the back of this book. J. W. White was a bookseller and stationer by trade, as well as being organist of the parish church at Mudeford.

The final event of the club year was the annual general meeting, held on 25 March 1878 in the club-room. Officers were elected (including the unanimous re-election of Captain Clarke) and eight new members were admitted. As the *Bournemouth Observer* put it "the Club now seems to be in a prosperous way, and we shall no doubt soon hear of its doings".

Monogram of the Christchurch Bicycle Club. It was produced as a silver-plated badge and worn on a polo cap. Every bicycle club would have its own badge.

10

2. Runs and races

THE OPENING run of the new season took place on a fine evening at the beginning of May in 1878, and was well supported:

The members of the Christchurch Bicycle Club made one of the most successful runs they have ever made on Thursday, 25 mustering at head quarters for a run to Lymington. A start was effected about 6.20 p.m., Mr. Ernest Clarke, the captain, leading the way and Mr. W. Burt, the sub-captain, bringing up the rear. A steady run through the town was made to Somerford, when the pace was somewhat increased. At Chewton, the stream caused a dismount. After a walk up the hill the signal for remounting was given, and a glorious run followed as far as Ashley Arnewood where it was found necessary to dismount, some of the younger members being unable to ride the steep and winding hill at this spot. This passed, they were soon again into the saddle, and a splendid run was then made into Lymington, which was reached at 7.30. A stay of some 17 minutes was made here for refreshment. At 7.47 the start for the return journey was made, the street was carefully ridden through, after which a sharp spin as far as Milton was done, when a halt was made, some members having failed to keep up the pace. This place was reached at 8.26, but not without a mishap, one young gentleman having experienced rather a heavy fall, another member had a severe attack of cramp, the latter being compelled to walk home. After a stay of about 20 minutes, another start was made for home the High Street being reached about 9.15, all being delighted with the ride.[19]

Another report contains some additional information. There were "twenty-two members and three friends" on this run. Milton (now New Milton) was reached at dusk and "those who had brought their lamps lit them". The roads were "all that could be desired the whole distance".[20]

The second report of the Lymington run also tells us that "most of the members wore their new uniform, which certainly improves the appearance of the riders". A photograph of the club taken the following year shows how this looked. Initially the suit was dark blue, but this was changed to brown early in 1880, at a general meeting of the riding members.[21] The club badge, a silver-plated monogram, was worn on the polo cap. The captain and sub-captain's caps were distinctive in having two lines around them. These gentlemen were also the only members to have bugles. In a number of clubs there was a special bugler, but this was apparently not so at Christchurch.

The cycling periodicals contain quite a lot of information on bugles and bugling. There were a number of calls employed to control club runs, the principal ones (according to the London Bicycle Club's bugler) being "the club call, assembly, mount, single file, double file, dismount, and the dinner or tea call".[22] These were commonly based on military bugle calls, but there was it seems no uniformity of practice. No less than ten calls were used by the Civil Service Bicycle Club, being reproduced for the information of readers in the *Bicycling Times* of 14 June 1877. Quite possibly some of these were noted and used by the Christchurch club.

After a "most delightful" evening run to Wimborne on 9 May, the next club event was another paper chase, again with Jenkins and Frampton as hares. It seems they won easily, as "the hares were only once seen, some of the best riders having lost the scent entirely during the whole of the run".[23] The following week, on the usual Thursday evening, a further opportunity was provided for the members to show their paces:

> *On Thursday evening, May 30, seventeen members mustered at head-quarters. After a ride of about two miles out of town the dismount was sounded, and the remainder of the evening was spent in some friendly racing between the members of the club. After a most enjoyable evening, home was reached at 9.15 p.m.*[24]

On Whit Monday the club took part in a 'meet', the jargon for a meeting of a number of bicycle clubs organised by a host club. The following season was to include a number of such events. This one was at Southampton:

> *On Whit Monday nine members started from headquarters for the run to Southampton, to take part in the meet held there. The route taken was via Lymington and Bewley to Hythe, at which place the steamer was taken, arriving at Southampton at 10.45 a.m. We at once proceeded to the South Western Hotel, where we were met by some members of the Chichester Club, who had just arrived. After a stroll round the town dinner was taken at the South Western Hotel at 1.30 p.m., between fifty and sixty riders sitting down, after which the parade took place, starting from the hotel, up the High Street, through the Bar, up the Avenue, and back, dismounting opposite the Hartley Institution. The start for the home journey was commenced at 4.15, accompanied by two members of the Chichester Club, who intended riding to Christchurch. The route chosen was via Lyndhurst and Brockenhurst, through the New Forest. Tea was taken at Lyndhurst, after which another start for home was made, arriving at Christchurch about 8.30 p.m., having had a most enjoyable day. C. W. Bollard, hon. sec.*[25]

Allowing for the ferry crossing at Southampton Water, this would have been a round trip awheel (excluding the parade) of about 46 miles. The muster of fifty to sixty would almost certainly have included other local clubs apart from the three named.

On the same day as the Southampton meet, the Bournemouth club were holding their first annual races at Dean Park. Four members of the Christchurch club attended and did well. Frampton won the one mile 'mounting and dismounting' race, whilst Jenkins won the hundred yards 'slow' race, each event obviously requiring special skills. The club's President, Sir Henry Woolf, was one of a "large concourse of spectators",[26] though whether in his official capacity or not is left unsaid.

A brief mention of the Bournemouth club seems appropriate at this point. It was formed in October 1877, fifteen months after the Christchurch Bicycle Club. It immediately took advantage of the already available facilities at Dean Park Cricket Ground and arranged the construction of a cinder track for racing purposes.[27] The annual Bournemouth Races, later coupled with a meet, became quite an event locally and continued for many years, indeed long after organised cycling at Christchurch had entirely ceased. In their book *Bournemouth* 1810–1910, published in the latter year, C. H. Mate and Charles Riddle tell us "Cycling and Athletics have always been popular in the district. The excellent ground at Dean Park has undoubtedly been the direct reason for this . . . The Bournemouth Bicycle Club held sports for twenty-four years in succession, until the general waning of athletics and cycling—principally the latter—some years ago compelled their cessation." *Kelly's Directory* confirms that the club continued in existence well into the Edwardian era.

The desirability of having a racing track was recognised also by the Christchurch club, the obvious site being the centrally-placed Barrack Road Recreation Ground. At the dinner in March 1878, Ernest Clarke had commented that "the Bournemouth Club were a little in advance of the Christchurch Club, in one sense; they had a cinder-track which Christchurch did not possess, but he hoped they would have one some day". There were cries of "hear, hear". Later the same year positive steps were taken to achieve this aim, an event being organised for the express purpose of augmenting "the fund for providing a special path for Bicyclists in the Recreation Ground".[28] At the 1879 dinner, "Mr. Jenkins, in responding for the racing members, said he thought it would be a good thing if a racing path could be obtained, as he felt sure there was some very good racing mettle in the club". The Mayor, George Ferrey (Ernest Clarke's father-in-law) commented "it would give him great pleasure to see a racing path in the recreation grounds if it could be made agreeable to the public generally, and if the matter came before the Corporation he should have great pleasure in supporting the project, but if it was done he was afraid the Corporation could not give much help from its funds, as they had already expended £400 on the ground".[29]

Sadly the dream never became a reality. Possibly there was opposition to the idea, perhaps insufficient funds were collected, or more likely (as we shall see later) were diverted to another purpose. Yet to this day the dream has not entirely faded from memory. The current (1935) byelaws, replacing earlier regulations of 1889, contain the following provision relating to recreation grounds within the borough:

> *Provided that, where the Council set apart a space in the pleasure ground for the use of bicycles, tricycles, or other machines, this byelaw shall not be deemed to prohibit the driving or wheeling to that space of a machine of the class for which it is set apart.*

But to return to our story. Whilst some members showed an interest in racing, the majority were quite happy simply to enjoy club runs. The easy three-mile country ride to the tiny village of Sopley was a good stand-by. The secretary reported:

> *The moonlight run to Sopley on Monday, 15th, was scantily attended only nine members putting in an appearance. At 8.40 p.m. a start was effected, and a pleasant ride ensued through Burton and Winkton. Sopley being reached, the usual dismount was sounded opposite the 'Wool Pack', where most of the members turned in, and had the usual refresher and a few songs. The captain also sang a very humerous song of his own composing, which kept the company in roars of laughter. After which the assembly was 'sounded', and a start made, arriving home about 10.10 p.m., having had a most enjoyable spin. Roads dusty; evening very fine.*[30]

Moonlight runs were a recognised club activity, more common of course during winter months. Although the two references to bugle calls ('dismount' and 'assembly') remind us of the quasi-military aspect of the organisation, it is quite clear that a far from regimental approach was adopted inside the 'Wool Pack'—and that the Captain was well able to entertain his troops. Unfortunately, we have no record of the song he composed, no doubt referring to the club's activities and members.

At the beginning of the next month, the club put aside their bicycles and took up cricket bats. A match was arranged against the Working Men's Institute Sports Club, and played on the Recreation Ground on Thursday evening, 1 August.[31] The Bicycle Club proved beyond doubt that this was not their sport, being bowled out for an ignominious 34 (the Captain getting a duck). The Sports Club got 99, Jenkins taking six wickets. We hear no more of cricketing.

A run at the end of August has historical interest. The club visited the Shakers at Hordle. They were an evangelical Christian group living in the area during the eighteen-seventies and eighteen-eighties, led by a spirited and spiritual lady known as Mrs. Girling. They suffered various trials and tribulations, and are frequently referred to in the local newspapers. At this particular time they had just been evicted from huts on land they had occupied as squatters, and had set up a very makeshift encampment on the highway. The cyclists' visit was reported as follows:

> *On Thursday, August 29th, a capital run was made to the Shakers at Hordle. Sixteen members turned up; a start was effected at 6.20 p.m., and a good pace was kept up through Newtown as far as Chewton-brook, where the signal for a dismount was given. This being passed, we were soon in the saddles again; at 7.15 we were in the midst of the community, and after a look round, an adjournment was made to the 'Bell Inn', where a stay of ten minutes was made for refreshments, after which a good run home was done via Milton, arriving at our destination about 8.35 p.m. The roads were in splendid going order, and the run was much enjoyed by all.*[32]

By a happy coincidence, the *London Illustrated News* sent down their artist the same month, and his drawings give an excellent impression of the scene "in the midst of the community".

During September there were four runs, three by moonlight, but the most exciting event took place at the end of the month:

> *On Thursday, 26th inst., an impromptu run was made to Bournemouth by several members to witness a mile race between E. W. Jenkins, of Christchurch Club, and R. Boxall, of the Bournemouth Club, Jenkins allowing Boxall twenty-five yards. The start was fixed for 5.45 p.m., but owing to a delay through Boxall breaking his pedal pin in a preliminary run round a start was not effected till a little after 6 p.m., when both men got off well together. In the first lap, Jenkins gained on his man considerably, and in the second he had caught him, and then a fine race ensued for the remaining two laps. Jenkins spurted three times, but Boxall gamely answered to it, and finally won by two yards. Time, 3 minutes 18 seconds. The race was run on the Bournemouth Cinder Track. Mr. J. Hayter, of the Bournemouth Club, officiated as starter and timekeeper.*[33]

Jenkins was undoubtedly the club's foremost racing man. For several years he travelled to races all over the South of England, often winning cups and other awards. At the annual dinner in 1880 the then ex-mayor Ferrey referred to him as "one amongst your number who has taken many prizes and is one of the best riders in this part of the country". The "racing gossip" column of *The Cyclist*, on 19 March 1882, noted that "Jenkins, of Christchurch, was also on the job at Taunton, but fell in his heat". Clearly he had a national reputation at this date—even if he occasionally fell down on the job!

On the same day as the Jenkins v. Boxall contest, there was a general meeting of about twenty members at the club-room in the High Street, to discuss two matters. We learn that "previous to this the papers and periodicals have been supplied by five or six individual members of the club".[34] The proposal was that each member living within a radius of a mile of the club-room should pay an additional shilling on top of his quarterly subscription of two shillings and sixpence. This would cover the cost of supplying papers (including no doubt the cycling periodicals quoted in this book) and other expenses. This was agreed. The old "papers, etc." were sold to members present for £1 7s. 11d. A discussion then took place as to "the advisability of getting a larger club room, the present room being too small for the increasing demands of the club". It was finally decided that the committee should take this step. As we shall see, this proved to be a mixed blessing.

Victorian Christchurch.   Beyond the River Avon lie the ruins of the Constable's House and Castle Keep.   Town Bridge is on the right.

16

Top: Ernest Clarke, the captain of the club, is in the foreground with his bugle. The others, left to right, are W. C. Sparkes, J. Frampton, A. J. Salter, R. Wheel, W. J. Payn, F. Cox, N. S. Newlyn, J. W. White. *Below:* F. Lane's tricycle (right) was worked by levers in this further photograph from 1879. Others, from the left, are W. Street, A. Street, H. Payn (with a dog that may have been the club mascot), W. Reeks and T. Gossling.

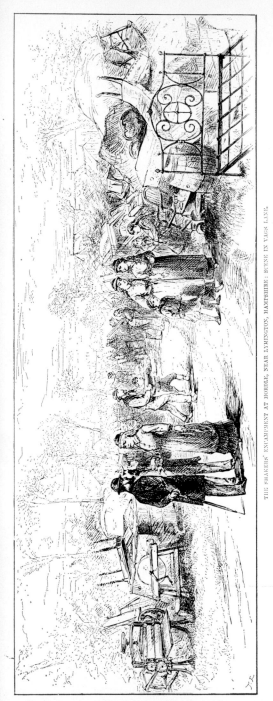

THE SHAKERS' ENCAMPMENT AT HORDLE, NEAR LYMINGTON, HAMPSHIRE: SCENE IN YAGS LANE.

The Shaker community at Hordle, August 1878.   Two drawings from the "London Illustrated News" show them after eviction.   Christchurch Bicycle Club rode out there to see what it was all about.

3. Fireworks and functions

THE CHRISTCHURCH Bicycle Club were obviously prepared to forgive the Sports Club for their ignominious defeat in the cricket match, for "on October 3rd, twenty-seven members attended the Annual Sports Club Dinner, at the Town Hall, at which 'Prosperity to the Christchurch Bicycle Club' was proposed by the Mayor (Mr. S. Bemister), and responded by Mr. E. Clarke, the captain. Dr. H. T. H. Mead also spoke of the interest he took in athletic sports, and he had engaged in all, he thought, but bicycling. He spoke highly of the Bicycle Club and the manner in which it was conducted, and he thought there were very few towns the size of Christchurch that had such a strong bicycle club". [35]

But if the club was strong, the committee still felt some incentive was necessary to keep up attendances at the moonlight runs planned for the winter months. Turnouts during the season had varied from a recorded maximum of twenty-five members to a minimum of seven: "At a committee meeting held on October 15, it was resolved that a cup be given to the member attending most club runs between November 7, 1878, and March 25, 1879, inclusive. In the event of a tie, the aggregate number of miles run to decide. Rule VII. to be strictly adhered to. It was also decided that the roll should be called immediately on arriving at the destination . . . As the above prize is given with a view of obtaining a larger muster than is usual at the meets, it is earnestly hoped that members will attend more regularly than hitherto". [36] We do not know what rule seven was about. It may have been a provision that members attend promptly for the start of runs. It was announced at the annual dinner the following March that Mr. V. Bradley won the award (a plain silver-plated tankard), but as he had left town a few days before, it was to be sent on to him.

Notwithstanding the carrot, the winter outings were not it seems very well supported. For example, "the run to Bransgore on Friday, 6th December, was very thinly attended, it being well-known the roads were in a bad state; in fact, nearly all the roads in the neighbourhood are more or less covered with stones or gravel". [37] Though despite "roads very rough" several members travelled to Bournemouth on 5 December to hear H. M. Stanley (who met Livingstone) deliver a lecture at the Town Hall. [38] The implication is that even if members were prepared to brave the "winter wind," the effect of rough weather on conditions underfoot—or rather underwheel—acted as a strong deterrent.

Frustrated to some extent in their riding ambitions, the members turned their energies at this time in other directions. For several years Guy Fawkes night had been used as an excuse in Christchurch and elsewhere for a display of hooliganism, with fireworks let off in the street and general disorder. The committee decided they should take the initiative and do something about this. A letter to the local newspaper gives their views:

Dear Sir. May we be allowed through the medium of the 'Christchurch Times', to acquaint its numerous readers and the public generally, that in order to celebrate the 5th of November in a proper manner, and to prevent the unruliness that sometimes prevails in Christchurch upon that evening, the Christchurch Bicycle Club has started a subscription list, for a display of fireworks to be held in the Recreation Ground, on Tuesday next, commencing at 8 o'clock. Subscriptions, fireworks, fuel, etc., will be thankfully received by the Committee of the Christchurch Bicycle Club. Hoping you will find space for the insertion of this letter. We are, dear sir, yours truly, Ernest Clarke, Captain,
C. W. Bollard, Hon. Sec.[39]

The event was a great success. The press reported it under the heading "What an Improvement!":

On Tuesday evening, the 5th instant, under the auspices of the Christchurch Bicycle Club, a large number of people gathered together in the public Recreation Ground, to witness the "proper manner to celebrate the fifth of November," when under the guidance of the captain of the club (Mr. Ernest Clarke), several pounds worth of fireworks were let off. Besides this, a monster bonfire was lighted, with a large 'guy' in the midst. Two or three tar barrels were brought upon the scene, the rolling of which created considerable amusement. During the evening two fire balloons (one 16, and the other 20 feet in circumference) were sent up. We think great praise is due to the club, for the letting off of fireworks in the street, was almost or entirely suspended, for most people took good advice, and went into the Recreation ground for their amusement.[40]

The secretary's own report estimates there were "over a thousand" persons present (the *Bournemouth Observer* suggests "several hundreds"), and adds that "the Captain, Mr. E. Clarke, deserves especial praise, for he worked like a horse".[41] The same month the club organised a concert. We first hear of this some time in advance of the event: "Bicycle Club Concert. The Bicycle Club here proposes to give its first concert in about a fortnight's time. Many of our amateur vocalists and pianists have kindly promised to assist, and the concert bids fair to be a very successful one".[42]

Two weeks later the local newspapers carry advertisements announcing "An Evening Concert will take place at the Town Hall, Christchurch, on Thursday next, November 21st 1878. Miss Maude Wilson (soprano) has been specially engaged". Further details followed, the price of tickets being stated to be: "reserved seats 2s., second seats 1s., promenade 6d."

The fullest report is in the *Bournemouth Observer*, but the secretary's own account gives the flavour well enough:

> *Our concert, which we gave in the Town Hall here on Thursday, the 21st inst., was in every way a success: in fact, every reserved seat was taken before the doors were opened. The programme, which was long and varied, was well rendered throughout. Miss Ferrey, Miss Wilson, and Miss King were heartily encored, as also was Mr. A. S. Reakes and Mr. E. W. Jenkins for their songs. The pianoforte duet by Mrs. J. E. Lane and Miss A. M. Davis, and the pianoforte solo by Mr. T. Holtham, were well received. The platform was tastefully decorated by Mr. and Mrs. E. Clarke. Mr. J. W. White kindly accompanied the songs, with the exception of Miss Ferrey's, which was played by Mr. Ferrey (the mayor). We can congratulate ourselves on this our first concert being financially successful, having cleared, after paying expenses, about seven guineas, which will be devoted to the fund for providing a special path for bicyclists in the Recreation Ground.*[43]

The next major social event was the club's second annual dinner on 19 March 1879. The decision had been made that this was to be held at the King's Arms Hotel, which from about this time became a regular venue for the club. The proprietor, N. S. Newlyn (twice mayor of Christchurch), obviously took a keen interest in the club's affairs, and is the bearded and hatted gentleman in a Christchurch Bicycle Club photograph that survives.

The annual dinner is fully reported in a number of places. It was "served in Mr. Newlyn's well-known style" and followed by a large number of speeches, toasts and songs. These include the Captain's rendering of J. W. White's adaption of the captain's song from 'H.M.S. Pinafore'[44] (see pages 55 & 56). The secretary, C. W. Bollard, said that the club "at the present time had 26 members"—about the same as the previous year—and that "during the past year there have been 30 club runs, in which a distance of over 400 miles had been ridden". He referred also to the success of the social events, to the usefulness of the club-room during the winter season, and the financial prosperity of the organisation—remarking that he had just deposited £15 at the Wilts and Dorset Bank to its credit. The report in the *Christchurch Times* concludes with the comment "the club is to be congratulated on its very flourishing condition".[45]

Perhaps the most staggering statistic to emerge from the reports of the dinner is that provided by the then sub-captain William Eaton Burt (later a solicitor in Bargates), speaking on behalf of the touring members. He said that "he had not done much touring in the last year, his longest run being 300 miles, but he had ridden altogether 4,380 miles, which was not the highest number ridden by a member, as Mr. Jenkins had completed 4,450 miles".

The reporter adds that "in a rather humerous speech he gave a little of his experience as a tourist and stated that he had bicycled in over 20 different countries, the longest run he had taken, having been to Leeds and back, a distance of 600 miles".[46] To sustain an average of more than 350 miles a month throughout the year, summer and winter, would be hard work on modern roads with today's machines. On the rough ways of a century ago, using bicycles with solid tyres, it was surely an amazing achievement.

As previously, the last event of the club year, the annual general meeting, took place on 25 March in the club-room, under the chairmanship of Captain Clarke. An important decision was made affecting the club's future. "The Chairman explained that a much larger and more convenient room had been offered to the club, and it was for the meeting to decide whether or not they should take it. It was then put to the meeting and carried unanimously 'that the secretary engage the room at once'."[47]

The new headquarters is shown in a contemporary line drawing, with the name of the club proudly displayed on four of the upper windows. The building still stands at the corner of Church Street and Castle Street, Christchurch. For a while, until its recent conversion to the Priory Tack Room, with flats above, the large first-floor club-room was free of modern trappings, and much how it must have looked a hundred years ago: "Illustrated and daily papers are supplied for the use of the members, and the room is nice and comfortably fitted-up. Mr. H. Pain presented the club with a billiard-board, and in addition, cards, boxing, fencing, and other games are allowed for the amusement and recreation of the members of the club".[48]

Members can be imagined perhaps dressed in club uniform after a run, talking, reading and playing the various games. Possibly they also drank beer obtained from a local pub or off-licence (this was the situation at Mudeford) but we cannot be sure of this.

Apart from the discussion on the club-room (which was actually entered on 3 May 1879), the general meeting dealt of course with the election of officers and committee members. It was also resolved "to present two cups to the members attending most club runs from March, 1879, to March, 1880", in other words during the forthcoming club year.

To encourage riding ability "the captain offered a cup to the member who rides during the same period without once having a fall".[49] We do not know whether anyone was able to claim this prize! At the end of the meeting "at the request of many members" the captain gave a further rendition of the adapted 'Pinafore' song, first sung at the annual dinner the previous week. One might say the year finished on a good note.

4. Local meets

AT THE beginning of the new season, a handful of members undertook an Easter tour of about 175 miles.

> *Five members started on Good Friday for Croydon; arrived at Alton after a trying pull against a strong head wind. Trained from Alton to Guildford, rode from Guildford to Leatherhead; again resorted to the train to Croydon. Riding distance, 65 miles. Saturday spent in town. Sunday rode from Croydon to Brighton in company with a member of the Saturn B.C.; arrived in Brighton 4.45, 44 miles. Easter Monday, started from Brighton 8.10 for home, via Chichester, Havant and Fareham; arrived at Southampton 2.32; 63 miles, including 1hr. 40 in stoppages; time in saddle a little under five hours. Wet through to the skin, we were compelled to train the remaining distance, 24 miles.*[50]

Perhaps the most notable feature of this report is the number of occasions on which the riders took advantage of the railway system to help them on their journey. In the 'Pinafore' parody the captain tells us "I'm never known to quail and come back home by rail"—but he of course qualifies this: "What, never?, No, never, What, never?, Well, hardly ever". Clearly discretion was occasionally the better part of valour.

There was a substantial increase in membership at the start of the 1879 season, partly due it seems to the acquisition of the new club-room. We are told: "the number of members of this club has largely increased of late, the club-room being now at the corner of Castle street".[51] The first few club runs were not particularly well attended, but on 8 May sixteen members and two friends had a "capital run to Lymington and back".[52] The following week also attracted the interest of members:

> *Bicycle Race. An exciting race took place on Wednesday morning, between a member of the Christchurch Bicycle Club (Mr. F. Cox), and one of the unattached (Mr. A. Howlett, Boscombe), the course being along the highway from Boscombe to Christchurch, a distance of nearly 3½ miles; after a very quick spin the club man lost the race, the unattached maintaining his start (about 400 yards) throughout. The winner was mounted on a 51 inch 'Excelsior', the club man on a 54 inch 'Humber'.*[53]

The types of machine used by club members at this time can be clearly seen from the photographs. One or two more sedate members rode tricycles, which had only been commercially produced a couple of years previously. The rest rode 'high' or 'ordinary' bicycles ('penny-farthings', as they later became known), no doubt by various different makers, there being a wide choice available. The size of the front wheel would probably have been between 48 inches and 56 inches, depending on the age, height and bravery of the individual owner. It appears from a photograph that Captain Clarke rode a large machine (probably 56 in.), whereas for example William Reeks used a much smaller one (probably 48 in.). At this date all the machines had straight handlebars, and of course solid rubber tyres. Braking was principally by pressure on the pedals attached by a crank to the front wheel, though some machines may have had a 'spoon' brake operating on the wheel (W. Reeks' machine appears to have such an attachment).

As the chapter heading suggests, 1879 can be regarded as the "year of the meets" so far as the Christchurch club is concerned. There had been one such event attended by the Christchurch club the previous season at Southampton and it may be the success of this prompted the club secretary to arrange a similar function locally. The *Christchurch Times* reported:

> *On Thursday evening last a meet of local bicycle clubs was held at Wimborne. Nine members of the Christchurch Bicycle Club started from the High Street (under the captaincy of Mr. W. Street sub-captain of the club) about 6 o'clock arriving at Wimborne 7 o'clock. The meet was arranged by the energetic secretary of the Christ-club (Mr. C. W. Bollard), he having written to the neighbouring clubs to arrange the meet, and at 7.30 the following clubs and numbers mustered in the Square:– Poole, 18 members, under the command of Captain Hansford; Bournemouth, 6 members, under the command of Captain Hayter; Ringwood, 6 members, under the command of Captain Waters; Christchurch, 9 members, under the command of Sub Captain Street; and about 12 unattached riders being in the rear. The riders—in all about 51—paraded the streets in single file under the command of Captain Hansford and dismounted in the Square. We may add that although such a large number of bicyclists met together in one town; the order kept was excellent and not one of them had a fall. The Christchurch members left Wimborne at 8.15 arriving at Christchurch at 9.15; and notwithstanding a strong north wind that was blowing, each journey was accomplished in an hour.*[54]

The following week saw a meet at Ringwood. Although the reports do not give the total numbers attending, we are told that ten Christchurch men had "a pleasant run and a jolly time with their brethren at the neighbouring town",[55] including "a pleasant hour at billiards at the Crown",[56] returning home about nine.

Now it was Christchurch's turn to play host, but unfortunately the weather was against them:

> *Under the auspices of this club a meet of bicyclists took place here*

on Monday last. Owing to the unpropitious state of the weather, the Ringwood club was the only local club that turned up. A procession was formed at 11.45 and a run through the principal streets was made whilst it was raining, which prevented many going in the run who intended to do so. After the run an adjournment was made to the Kings Arms for luncheon, provided by host Newlyn in his usual excellent style. A vote of thanks was accorded to the Ringwood club for their attendance on such an unfavourable day. Between 30 and 40 took part in the procession. By kind permission of Mr. Newlyn, a photograph of the Christchurch club was taken by Mr. Cobb, in the grounds opposite the hotel.[57]

On the afternoon of the same day as the Christchurch meet (Whit Monday, 2 June 1879) the Bournemouth club held their annual races, despite the fact that the weather continued to be "about as unfavourable as it well could be, a drenching rain falling nearly the whole of the day". Jenkins and Frampton attended from Christchurch, the former being unplaced in a five-mile handicap race. J. B. Fampton got through to the final of the two-mile bicycle race, which is vividly reported:

A good start was effected, and after some hard riding, at the third lap the positions of the men were:— Frampton, 1; Lane, 2; Hayter, 3; Street, 4; Keynes, 5; Metcalfe, 6. In the fourth lap Hayter passed Lane, and began to close up to Frampton. The latter, however, had plenty of spurting power left in him, and beginning to realise that Hayter, who was looked upon by many as a certain winner, was drawing close to him, put on a splendid spurt, and increased the distance between himself and the favourite opponent. In the fifth lap the position of the competitors remained the same as in the preceding lap; but in the sixth lap Metcalfe, who rode exceedingly well, passed Street, with whom he had been spurting for some time, and thus placed himself third, a position he maintained to the finish. Hayter and Frampton raced well together, and in the seventh lap the former began again to draw close upon Frampton who, however, in turn put on another good spurt and increased his lead considerably. As there was now only one more lap to run, it became evident that Hayter had got his work well cut out to make a win of it. He put on a tremendous spurt, which was answered to by Frampton, who, however, began to lose ground. Both men now strove their utmost, but Frampton, after a hard struggle, came in winner, about 12 yards in front of Hayter, who had made it warm work for him. Metcalfe was a good third, being only some 30 yards behind the second man. Time of winner, 7m. 10secs.[58]

According to another report, Frampton's prize was a silver cup. He went on to win a "closely contested" one-mile mounting and dismounting race (as he had the year before), the prize this time being a silver-mounted combination inkstand. He must have been well pleased with his day.

Another meet took place in Ringwood on 12 June, with three other clubs in attendance (Ringwood, Wimborne and Poole), Christchurch providing eighteen of the thirty-two riders.[59] The following week produced a "monster meet" at Poole, with the clubs present (Poole, Christchurch, Bournemouth, Ringwood, Blandford, Wimborne) mustering 93 members in all, "the rear being brought up by 18 unattached riders and 6 tricycles, including a lady tricyclist, who proved herself no novice, and managed the Salvo in admirable style".

This is an early date for a female cyclist, and one admires her all the more for venturing alone (it would seem) with 116 men! As the procession passed the Poole headquarters the second time round it encountered the Salvation Army and their captain, another independent lady "known in Poole as 'Hallelujah Emmer', singing lustily, "See the mighty host advancing, Satan leading on", causing much merriment and considerable obstruction".[60]

On 24 June a special general meeting was held, only briefly reported in the local press with the enigmatic comment "a few alterations in the rules made".[61] We can only guess what these may have been. Possibly the substantial increase in numbers included a large number of non-riders, and it was thought advisable to make provision for two classes of membership. We know that at some stage this took place, since there is a reference the following year to a general meeting of the "riding members".[62]

Jenkins and Frampton (and three others) were off to Bournemouth again on 26 June to take part in the Athletic Sports, the former winning the mile race and the latter the three-mile one.[63] But the event of the year was undoubtedly the Christchurch meet held on the evening of 10 July. It was larger even than the Poole meet the month before, and is given full coverage in both the local and cycling press. The *Christchurch Times* reported:

Bicycle Meet at Christchurch. Under the auspices of the Christchurch Bicyle Club, a sight not often seen took place here on Thursday evening last, namely; that about one hundred and forty bicycles with riders—properly termed a meet—assembled at the clubroom, in the market square. The meet was timed at 6 o'clock, and between six and seven, members of the Bournemouth, Blandford, Lymington, Mudeford, Poole, Ringwood and Wimborne began to put in an appearance, with several unattached riders. At about a quarter to seven a procession was formed, headed by the Christchurch club, and a start made round the town in the following order:– Christchurch, under the command of Captain E. Clarke; Bournemouth, Capt. Hayter; Poole, Capt. Hansford; Ringwood, Capt. Waters; Blandford, Capt. Hanks; Wimborne, Capt. Lane;

The club-room was above Froud's
shoe shop, at the corner of Church
Street and Castle Street in Christchurch.
The name of the club appears on the
first-floor windows.   From the outside
the building looks much the same today.

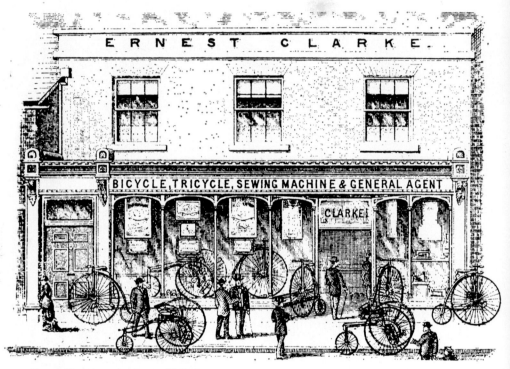

Ernest Clarke's cycle shop.   All kinds
of Victorian everyday bicycles, as well
as tricycles, are on display in the window
and along the pavement.   It was a
lively scene.

Lymington, Capt. Purchase; and Mudeford, under the captaincy of Captain Last, and whose uniform was very natty, the rear being brought up by almost forty unattached riders. Several hundreds of persons assembled at the lower part of the High Street, the Market Square, and in Castle Street. The band of the 10th Hants Rifle Volunteers, enlivened the evening by playing a selection of music in front of the Hotel. The route of the procession (which was nearly a half mile in length), was from the Hotel through High Street, West End, Bargates, and Stour Road, thence to Mudeford, Bure Homage by Humphreys and Somerford bridges, down Street Lane, through the town to West End and then to the Hotel, where the dismount was made, and the various clubs were entertained by Host Newlyn. After luncheon the clubs went to Mr. Newlyn's bowling green, where it was arranged that the next meet should take place at Bournemouth at an early date. Cheers were given to the Christchurch captain, those present, and the band, when the clubs started for their destinations shortly before nine. The following is the official statement of the various clubs present with their numbers:– Christchurch, 30; Bournemouth, 10; Poole, 17; Blandford, 8; Wimborne, 8; Lymington, 11; Mudeford, 5; making a total of 96 attached members; there was also 32 unattached members and eight tricycle riders, bringing the total up to 136. [64]

Other reports provide additional tit-bits of information, such as that "by the kind permission of Mr. Newlyn the Castle Green was placed at the disposal of the club, and on the arrival of each club and unattached bicyclists the machines were piled up in regular order" and "the town presented a very lively appearance on account of the bunting spread across the street in various places". [65]

The *Bicycling News* report of 18 July contained a compliment: "The Christchurch club is generally acknowledged to be the best in the neighbourhood, and a very warm and kindly feeling is entertained towards it by other clubs in the district, and the Christchurch men having been hearty and enthusiastic in their support of meets held in other towns, it was confidently anticipated that their kindness would be reciprocated, and that the muster on this occasion would be a very large one."

Although further meets took place during July and August at Bournemouth, Blandford, Poole and Ringwood, it seems none was numerically anything like as successful as the Christchurch one. The second Poole meet took place at the residence of the Reverend J. L. Williams at Stanley Green, where after a short run machines were piled on the lawn "where tables were laden with lemonade, sherry, beer, tea, coffee, cake, etc. ad lib". [66] Enough, one would think, to quench the thirst of the most parched high-wheeler.

Throughout this period the club's foremost racing member,

E. W. Jenkins, was continuing to enhance his reputation at meetings all over the south of England—presumably travelling by train to save his energy. He won first prizes at places as far apart as Crewkerne, Chichester, Yeovil and Taunton. His collection of cups and other awards must by now have been quite impressive. But he was by no means the only energetic member. We have mentioned W. E. Burt's impressive touring mileage the previous year, and Frampton's successes at Bournemouth. We now learn that "Mr. C. W. Bollard of the Christchurch Bicycle Club has recently ridden 130 miles in one day being we understand the longest distance yet covered by any member of the Christchurch Bicycle Club".[67] This put him on the "hundred mile list", a much-sought achievement in the early days of cycling.

Only a few moonlight runs are recorded during the autumn of 1879, and these were not particularly well supported. On the social side, a number of members once again attended the Sports Club dinner at the Town Hall on 2 October, wearing their uniform. As before, a toast to "the Bicycle Club" was proposed by Mr. Bemister and replied to by Captain Clarke.[68] And as in the previous year— but with variations:

> *The Fifth of November was celebrated in the Recreation Ground, under the auspices and direction of the Bicycle club, who undertook to collect contributions for the purpose, and superintended the arrangements, which included a torch-light procession round the ground, a bonfire, and a display of rockets and other fireworks. The 10th Hants Band was in attendance and to its strains dancing was kept up for a time.*[69]

The winter scene is described well by the club's secretary in the February 1880 issue of *Cycling:*

> *The club is steadily on the increase, numbering now nearly sixty members. We have a large club-room, centrally situated, in which we have two billiard tables, which have kept the members well together during the winter months. We have had but few club runs of late, the roads in the neighbourhood, in all directions, being covered with stones or gravel; but skating has been freely indulged in by the members. Christchurch Harbour, fifteen minutes walk from the club-room, is at the present time almost entirely frozen over, which is a rare treat in this part of the country.*

Ernest Clarke, in his role of retailer, was quick to satisfy the current need. Three issues of the *Christchurch Times* during December 1879 contained an advert for his firm: "Skating. For skates go to Clarke & Lawrence, Christchurch. Skates ground and repaired".

The club's third annual dinner took place at "Newlyn's Hotel" (the King's Arms) on 10th February, 1880. It was well attended and

26

presided over by the Mayor, Henry Pain, who was thanked by the Captain "for the present of the billiard table which he had made to the club since the last year. The Mayor, in responding, paid a tribute to the excellent and thoroughly respectable manner in which the club was conducted". The secretary responded to the toast "Success to the Christchurch Bicycle Club" (proposed by the ex-mayor George Ferrey) stating that the club had increased its membership during the year from about thirty to nearly sixty. He said there had been about twenty club runs during the year, about three hundred miles having been travelled, and referred to the success of the meet and the fireworks display. He explained that a second billiard table had been bought by the members, adding that the previous year they had had £15 in hand "but that had been taken out of the bank in order to help pay for the new billiard table, on which there still remained a debt of about £25".[70] So much for the racing track fund!

As usual, there was plenty of singing at the 1880 dinnner. J. W. White sung another song he had composed, entitled simply *The C.B.C.* Only the chorus survives (reproduced on page 56), but we are told that in the verses the members "certainly not lacking in self-appreciation" were made to extol themselves as being "handsome, good, and true, graceful and fast riders, and crack billiard shots". The song was "rapturously encored".[71]

And on the subject of appreciation:

Mr. W. A. Marshall proposed 'the health of the Captain'—(loud applause)—who he said had worked hard in the interests of the club and to whom a large portion of its success was due. He referred to the fact that Mr. Clarke was always re-elected without the slightest opposition and testified to his graceful riding and his constant urbanity towards the members of the club. He presented Mr. Clarke, on behalf of the members, with a handsome jug of oak, enammeled interior, and silver mountings. Upon the lid was the inscription, 'Presented to Edward Ernest Clarke, captain of the Christchurch Bicycle Club, by the members, Feb. 10th 1880'. The Captain suitably responded, and subsequently proposed 'The Sub-Captain, Secretary and Committee', paying a high compliment to the way in which the secretary performed his arduous duties and presenting that official with a black leather writing case. Mr. Bollard appropriately replied, and other complimentary toasts followed.[72]

On 24 March 1880 the annual general meeting took place in the club-room. The secretary read the balance sheet "which showed the club to be in a very prosperous condition, the receipts for the year being about £120". All the principal officers were re-elected, and other positions filled, and "it was decided to ask the Rev. Z. Nash to become vice-president".[73] The Reverend Zachary Nash, vicar of Christchurch Priory since 1871 to his death in 1883, was chairman of the Sports Club and obviously took an interest in local sporting activities. He had accepted the vice-presidential nomination. The club now had the best possible "moral support".

ERNEST CLARKE
BICYCLE AGENCY,
MILLHAMS STREET, AND ALBERT VILLA
PUREWELL, CHRISTCHURCH.

Ariel, Swiftsure, Tangent, Excelsior, Rudder Excelsior Duplex Excelsior, Premier, Paragon, Speedwell, Suspension, Combination, Safety, Challenge, Coventry Racer, Gentleman's, Pegasus, London, Coventry Champion, Invincible, Centaur, Coventry Triumph, Shadow, Humber, &c.

India Rubber Tyred Carriage and Perambulator Wheels Saddles, Cement, Wrenches, Oil Cans, Bells, Valises, Lamps, and all appliances for Bicycles.

Bicycles for learners free of charge.   Bicycles repaired.

BICYCLES OF EVERY DESCRIPTION BOUGHT SOLD, OR EXCHANGED.
EASY TERMS OF PAYMENT IF DESIRED.

28

5. Declining years

THE NEW season started well with the Lymington run on 22 April 1880. Indeed there was an affirmation of the entente cordiale between the two Christchurch clubs: "Twelve members attended the opening run for Lymington, in company with eight members of the Mudeford B.C. Roads splendid".[74] The following month fifteen members rode to Bournemouth for the first Whit Monday meet there.[75] This was attended by a large number of clubs and is graphically described in a supplement to *The Cyclist* for 26 May:

> *About 150 bicyclists visited the town, including representatives from the Pickwick, Christchurch, Mudeford, Ringwood, Wandering Minstrels (Wimborne), Poole, Castle Wanderers (Sturminster Newton), Clapham, Basingstoke, Portsmouth, Southampton Amateurs, Winchester and County, Shaftesbury, Fareham, Isle of Wight, South Hants, Brixton Ramblers and other clubs. The procession started shortly after two o'clock, the bicyclists walking down the hill as far as the London Hotel, and proceeding along the Exeter-road to the sands, thence up the Bath-hill and round by the Westover Gardens, again returning to the Square. Owing to the great crowd assembled, some difficulty was experienced in turning here, and the riders had for the second time to dismount, having previously done so at the beach.*

The procession then made its way to the Dean Park Cricket Ground for the annual races.

The ubiquitous Jenkins was much in evidence at the Bournemouth races, though his ability was it seems over-estimated by the organisers:

> *A circumstance which was noticed perhaps as much as anything in the arrangements of the programme was the heavy handicapping, or in other words the comparatively small chances which Messrs. Hansford and Jenkins, for instance, as scratch men, had of overtaking their opponents, though in themselves first class riders.*

This resulted in Jenkins being unplaced in either the one or three-mile handicap races. However the final contest was a straight ten-mile race between just two competitors, and was most exciting:

> *A great deal of interest was attached to this, the last bicycle race on the programme, the prize being a medal indicating the year's championship of the Bournemouth Bicycle Club. Two competitors started—R. Boxall and E. W. Jenkins. The race lasted for forty minutes, and the contestants passed each other several times, keeping well together throughout the race. There were 37¾ laps to the ten miles, and in the 34th lap, a little anxiety was felt owing to a defect in the machine which was ridden by Jenkins, and which*

29

the rider twice complained of as he passed the judge, seeming for a little time to be disheartened by the fact. For a lap or two Boxall, by putting on a few spurts, was enabled, at this critical period of the race, to get some distance ahead, but Jenkins, notwithstanding the temporary defect in his machine, which he described as "something the matter", drew up to his opponent again, and was heartily cheered as he ran a neck and neck race in the 35th lap. In the next round, however, Jenkins got a start of three or four yards, but was again caught by Boxall, and, whereas the riders were neck and neck when half way round the last lap, Jenkins put on a magnificent spurt and almost 'flew' into the winning post amid the cheers of the assembly, and several yards in front of his opponent.[76]

The winner's medal indicated "the year's championship of the Bournemouth Bicycle Club", the implication being that E. W. Jenkins was a member. From reports of one or two other events this appears to be correct. It was quite possible for a keen wheelman to belong to more than one club. In fact, Jenkins is almost invariably referred to as being of the Christchurch club, and this was obviously his primary allegiance. It was indeed under these colours that he won races at Lillie Bridge (beating the famous Cortis) and Stamford Bridge the same month.[77]

On 20 May six members had a run to Wimborne ("roads very loose and stony"[78]), but the next recorded major event was the Christchurch meet on 24 June. As on the first occasion they had played host the previous year, the club was unlucky with the weather:

On Thursday a bicycle meet took place opposite the Hotel, under unprecedented difficulties. At six o'clock, owing to the inclement weather there were not many present, but, one by one, the clubs came in, and the following clubs were represented:– Christchurch, Bournemouth, Bournemouth Grosvenor, Chichester, Blandford, Mudeford, Ringwood, Wimborne Minster, and the Wandering Minstrels (Wimborne). After a little while, a procession was formed, which proceeded through the principal streets of the town during a downpour of rain, after which they had some refreshment and departed homewards. The Rifle band was in attendance and played a selection of music in the Castle Street during the evening.[79]

From another report we learn there were some seventy riders in attendance. Bearing in mind that (as one report puts it) "rain set in during the early part of the afternoon" this was a very fair turnout, though according to the secretary "all the clubs for 30 miles around" had promised to be present.

On the day after the Christchurch meet C. W. Bollard resigned as honorary secretary, a post he had held since the early days of the club's existence. His reason for doing so was that he was leaving town, possibly for London (where he attended a meeting as the club's representative the following year). On 5 July "a complimentery dinner was given by the Christchurch club".[80] There can be little doubt that the loss of such an energetic and conscientious secretary was sorely felt by the club. Although we have no reason to suppose that his successor, W. E. Burt (the touring member), failed to carry out his duties, it is surely significant that the reports of the club's doings in the cycling periodicals almost entirely cease from this moment onwards.

The only recorded cycling activity during the second half of 1880, and indeed for the remainder of the club year, was a trip to attend the Ringwood meet on 24 August:

> *The clubs represented were Ringwood, Christchurch, Bournemouth, Lymington, Wandering Minstrels and Bournemouth Grosvenor. A procession was formed at 7 o'clock which paraded the town, the Ringwood club, who had an excellent muster and looked well in their new dark green uniform, leading the way. The Christchurch, Lymington and Bournemouth Grosvenor also were well represented. After parading the town all riders were invited to partake of refreshments in the Town Hall, provided by the home club.*[81]

The total number attending was reported as 66, including tricyclists.

What is not clear is whether the number of club runs and meets did reduce to a mere handful during the 1880–81 season, from an average of something like one a fortnight during the previous two years, or whether they simply ceased to be reported. The answer probably lies somewhere between the two alternatives. Although the various meets had made the 1879 season a successful one, the actual number of runs done had decreased somewhat. Possibly the members began to tire of following the same limited number of routes from the town centre, particularly when the new club-room provided such a counter-attraction. Nevertheless, the recorded events for 1880 show reasonable attendances (with the exception of the Wimborne run), and it seems fair to assume that there must have been at least a few runs not noticed by the local press, and not reported to the cycling periodicals by Bollard's successor.

The importance of the club's headquarters at this stage can be gathered from an advertisement in the local press: "The Committee of the Christchurch Bicycle Club require a person to take charge of the Club Room. Applications to be addressed to the Secretary, not later than the 31st instant".[82] No satisfactory response was obtained, for the advert was repeated three weeks running at the end of September and beginning of October, when presumably the post was either filled or the committee made other arrangements.

However successful or otherwise the 1880 cycling season may have

been, the club, as on the two previous occasions, made a fine show-
ing on the Fifth of November. This year they advertised in the local
press: "Guy Fawkes Day. The Christchurch Bicycle Club would be
glad to receive RUBBISH for FUEL for the BONFIRE in the Recreation
Ground on the 5th November. Notice should be given to the
Secretary, who will then send cart". [83] According to the *Christchurch
Times* the club had this year "proposed, carried, contemplated, tried
and succeeded in a celebration upon a larger scale", that was described elsewhere as follows:

> *The Fifth of November passed off quietly in Christchurch, there
> being a demonstration, consisting of a torchlight procession and
> subsequent bonfire, organised by the members of the Christchurch
> Bicycle Club, who carried out their programme in a spirited manner,
> creating no disorder. At about half-past six o'clock a procession
> was formed in Wick Lane, where about a hundred torches and blue
> lights were distributed, and the principal streets of the town were
> paraded. The procession was headed by a few members of the
> Rifle Volunteer Band, and after perambulating the town, thereby
> creating a good deal of interest, they proceeded to the Recreation-
> ground where a large bonfire was ignited, and a very creditable
> display of fireworks took place. After a lengthened period of great
> enjoyment for those who favoured the proceedings with their patro-
> nage the assembly dispersed. We may mention that in the bonfire
> about 500 faggots were used, and about a dozen tar barrels assisted
> materially the effect of the conflagration. At about ten o'clock,
> after a number of songs had been sung, the crowd, before dispersing
> sang the National Anthem. Everything passed off in a satisfactory
> manner.* [84]

Nothing further is heard of the club until the following spring.
Very probably the members had by this time given up winter runs,
which had never been particularly popular. Moreover, there is no
report of the annual dinner. This may well have taken place as
usual in February or March, but passed unobserved by the local
papers. At the annual general meeting on 29 March 1881, W. C.
Sparkes took over from W. E. Burt as honorary secretary, and as a
first task reported the meeting to the cycling periodicals. [85] It was
at this meeting that it was unanimously resolved to join the Bicycle
Union (now the British Cycling Federation). Better late than never,
as the saying goes. C. W. Bollard attended a meeting at the Man-
chester Hotel in London on 13 October of the same year. [86] The
secretary put in a plaintive report of a run to Wimborne at the
beginning of the new season (12 May 1881):

> *Only two members of this club turned up for the run to Wimborne
> on Thursday last, via Bournemouth, which club we were to have
> met at their headquarters, but they even failed to turn out a rider.*

32

The roads, which are in a most wretched condition, must be the cause of such a poor muster. The club has decided to give the bicyclist and tricyclist a cup or prize, value two guineas, that attends most runs during the year, which I hope will induce members to turn up more numerously. [87]

The attempt to sustain numbers by offering an attendance cup had been made on previous occasions. Whether at this stage it was in any way successful is open to doubt.

But despite an apparently sharp decline in the club's riding activities, the third annual meet was held on 8 September 1881, and proved to be a most lively affair:

Owing probably to the fact that the meet had been postponed, it having been originally advertised to take place on an earlier date, there were not quite so many cyclists as on former occasions, but seldom have so fine a body of men as well mounted been seen at any similar gathering in this part of the country. From five o'clock in the afternoon riders began to pour into the town from all parts, so that at a quarter to six the old Market Square presented a very animated appearance. About ten minutes before six the bugle call was heard and almost immediately the stalwart form of the Captain of Christchurch Club was seen leading off the procession. The manner in which the start was made was much admired, each rider falling into his place in the line with the utmost precision. The procession passed through the town as far as Bargates, back to Purewell Cross, and thence to the Club-room, where the visitors were entertained with substantial fare. The line of the route was profusely decorated with bunting, as was also the Christchurch Club-house. To the indefatigable efforts of Mr. E. Clarke (captain), and Mr. Sparkes (hon. sec.), must be attributed the great success which attended the meet. The following clubs were largely represented: Christchurch, Ringwood, Poole, Bournemouth, Parkstone and Wimborne. [88]

As in the previous year, one is tempted to think that if (inter alia) the Christchurch club was "largely represented" and still able to organise such a successful meet, there must have been some summer runs ignored by the local press and unreported to the cycling periodicals.

With the advent of autumn, the arrangements for Guy Fawkes night had to be considered. It seems the committee decided there would be too much work involved in trying to repeat the previous year's entertainment, for we read that "the Bicycle Club has decided not to hold a demonstration on the 5th of November this year, as they have done hitherto". [89]

We can take it that the winter months were spent within the cosy confines of the club-room. We read: "On Thursday last the Christchurch Bicycle Club received their new billiard table (valued at eighty-five guineas) from Messrs. Wright & Co., of London. The club has now two full-sized tables in use".[90] Presumably one of the two tables acquired earlier was now thought to be too small. But eighty-five guineas was a lot of money nearly a hundred years ago, especially for a modest-sized club with an unaltered annual membership subscription of just fourteen shillings. There can be little doubt where the members' priorities now lay.

N.S.NEWLYN'S FAMILY HOTEL,

POST HORSES & MODERN BUILT CARRIAGES   CHRISTCHURCH, HANTS   AGENT TO THE S.W. RAILWAY COMPANY

IMPORTER & DEALER IN FOREIGN WINES & SPIRITS

An Omnibus serves all the Trains f.m London for Bournemouth except the 5.10 P.M. Tr.? f.m Waterloo   And Omnibuses f.m every T.n to the Kings Arms

SEE ADVERTISEMENT AT THE END OF BOOK

Kings Arms Hotel, used by the club for dinners and other functions. As it was about a hundred years ago, much as it is today.

6. Metamorphosis

OF THE summer of 1882 we know nothing so far as the Christchurch Bicycle Club is concerned. It is on record that Jenkins was still taking part in races, at Taunton, Southampton and Bournemouth, where he won the three-mile handicap on Whit Monday.[91] But of the club's activities we are ignorant. It is possible that there were one or two runs by the remaining riders, but this is mere conjecture. Although it seems the club membership never fell below about fifty from 1880 onwards, we must assume that the majority of these were non-riding, having probably joined to enjoy the social and indoor sporting facilities of the club-room.

There is no reason to suppose that any dramatic event occurred, say, during the early part of 1882, resulting in a decision by the club or its committee that there should be no further cycling activities. We can take it that the metamorphosis was a gradual one. The early bicyclists and tricyclists had done it all and drifted away to try something new, or stayed in the club but allowed their machines to grow rusty. Some may have left to join more virile clubs elsewhere in the area. The mistake was, it seems, in allowing the social side—and the billiards—to develop at the expense of the club's primary object, without attempting to build up a new generation of keen young riders.

So the year passed with not a single run recorded. Perhaps surprisingly, the annual general meeting on 29 March 1883 was reported in one of the local papers. We find that:

> *The annual meeting of the bicycle club was held in the club-room, on Thursday, Mr. E. E. Clarke presiding. The balance sheet, which was adopted, showed the club funds were in a healthy state. The whole of the officers were re-elected for the ensuing year. A vote of thanks to the chairman concluded the proceedings. About 20 members were present.*[92]

It is an enigmatic report which says nothing of what had come to pass. The uniformed reader could be excused for thinking that little had changed at this stage. Ernest Clarke presided, there was a healthy bank balance, all officers were re-elected, and a vote of thanks was given to the chairman. The true picture, however, so far as bicycling activities were concerned, emerges the following month.

"The Bicycle Club have been invited to take part in the proposed meet at Bournemouth on Whit Monday, *but as there are so few riders in the club*", (our emphasis) "the representatives (if any) will not be numerous".[93] We do not know whether any of the "few riders" put in a final appearance at Bournemouth or not, though it is on record that the sports "were not very largely attended".[94]

By the winter of 1883 the metamorphosis was complete. We are told that: "a billiard handicap has been started at the Bicycle Club. There were 20 entries".[95] This continued for about a month, since "a billiard handicap at the Bicycle Club was brought to a close on Wednesday evening, when Mr. Herbert Reekes, who was the limit man, proved himself the victor. Messrs. E. Clarke and E. W. Jenkins were second and third respectively. Some of the games were very closely contested".[96] The interesting point is of course that both Clarke and the club's leading racing man, E. W. Jenkins, continued to take a full part in its activities even after cycling had gone out of fashion. This tends to confirm (as did the annual meeting) that there had been no major split in the club between the cycling members and the others.

Although the next annual general meeting, for 1884, is not reported, a later entry suggests it was probably at this time that Ernest Clarke was finally replaced as chairman by C. Aldridge. No doubt the meeting also discussed the club's future as a non-cycling body, for in April we read the following comment in the local paper: " 'What's in a name?' What was formerly known as a 'Bicycle' club, and which has dwindled down from the practice of bicycle-riding to the less innocent, but more harmless, occupation of billiard-playing is, it is said, about to replace the word 'bicycle' in its title, by the name of 'Twynham'. Would it not be advisable to sink the antiquarian, and to call a spade a spade"?[97]

The newspaper's advice was not taken, as the old name for Christchurch was adopted as the new name of the club on 7 May 1884, just short of eight years after its original formation: "The Twynham Club. A special general meeting of the members of the Twynham Club (late the bicycle club) was held in the club room on Wednesday evening, Mr. C. Aldridge presiding. There was a good attendance of members. Amongst other business the new rules were submitted and passed".[98]

The reconstituted organisation remained in existence, initially with W. C. Sparkes as secretary, for quite a number of years indeed until around the turn of the century,[99] but its history is not our concern. That "enthusiastic little country club"[100], the Christchurch Bicycle Club, was no more.

But we can end this chapter, and the main history of the club, on a more philosophical note, with an editorial comment from *Wheel World* of November 1883:

Some well-known bicycle clubs of a few years ago have dwindled

The Coventry Tricycle is sometimes termed "our first modern tricycle". Ernest Clarke was selling them in 1877. They were reasonably comfortable and easy to ride. This is a Science Museum photograph

away to nothing; and of others, once on everybody's lips, there is nothing heard. This would be alarming but for one fact, and that is that just as some large clubs have gone down so have others come up; and today, cycling, as far as clubdom alone even is concerned, is just as prosperous as ever it was.

The era of the bicycle clubs continued throughout the 1870s and 80s. By the early 1890s the pneumatic-tyred safety bicycle was well-established and cycling became extremely popular at all levels of society. This was so in Christchurch as elsewhere, and indeed from 1892 onwards the *Christchurch Times* published a regular series of "cycling notes". The early issues refer in passing to the rambles of a newly-formed Christchurch Cycling Society, which had had its inaugural meeting in February 1892, under the presidency of F. A. Lane, previously a tricycling member of the old bicycle club.

The indications are that the new society may have been short-lived, though as the local issues of the paper for 1893 to September 1896 are missing we cannot speak with any certainty. From the end of 1896 the cycling notes continue in a more general form, with no references to any local club or activities. From September 1903 they are headed "Cycling and Motoring", and cease altogether at the beginning of 1905. A faster, noisier machine now took precedence on the roads of England. The golden years were over.

OPPOSITE: the Flying Dutchman was one of the new rotary tricycles featured in Clarke and Lawrence's 1879 advertisement (left). Later there was local competition. The William Jeans advertisement (right) began to appear in the papers after he had branched out on his own.

7. Clarke the cycle seller

ERNEST CLARKE had early business connections in Christchurch with the watch fusee-chain manufactory originally started by Robert Harvey Cox and carried on through the 19th century by his descendants, mentioned in a book by Allen White, *The Chain Makers*, published in 1967. Further research is necessary, but it would appear that the business was disposed of by Price W. Cox (trading as P. W. Cox & Co. in 1867) to a partnership which included Ernest's father, William, of Coventry. The suggestion is that Ernest was employed for a time as manager.

Shortly after the formation of the bicycle club, our Captain married a local girl at the Priory Church. The *Christchurch Times* contains the following item:

> *Interesting presentation. The workpeople at Mr. Clarke's watch-chain manufactory, have presented Mr. Ernest Clarke with a cut glass biscuit basket and a pair of sugar tongs, for the purchase of which they had subscribed, on the occasion of his marriage with Miss Charlotte Ferrey, second daughter of Mr. George Ferrey, of Christchurch.* [101]

George Ferrey was Mayor of Christchurch in 1878.

Ernest started his own cycle agency business in 1873—as a number of his later adverts proudly proclaim. He traded from various addresses, but from about September 1876 began to use the Millhams Street workshop, at the back of the High Street premises occupied by the watch-chain manufactory. The latter business was probably by now in decline, for twelve months later we discover a notice of dissolution of the partnership: "W. Clarke, W. J. Hyley and F. Bayley, as Cox & Co., watch, fuzee, and chain manufacturers, Christchurch, Hants". [102] Though it should be added that as late as January 1877 there is an advertisement: "Clarke's Chain Factory. Wanted. A competent person to teach children to Rivet, and to look after their work generally". [103]

Edward Ernest was once described in the local paper as "our enterprising bicycle agent". [104] He certainly advertised widely, and was quick to promote any new machine appearing on the market. His 1876 advertising shows that he was able to supply a wide variety of bicycles. By December of the same year he was also advertising as a repairer. The following June he altered his "bicycles for learners 5s. a week" to "bicycles for learners free of charge", no doubt with a view to increased future sales. In September 1877 we read: "A Novelty. Mr. E. Clarke, the local bicycle agent, has just introduced into Christchurch the 'Coventry Tricycle' which is quite a novelty in Velocipedes and one likely to prove a most valuable means of locomotion". This has been called "the first modern tricycle" and was worked by levers. The author has one of the few surviving examples, on which he has ridden several hundred miles.

In July 1878 we find Ernest "Selling Off!! Selling Off!! Present Stock of Bicycles at a Great Reduction. Ernest Clarke, Bicycle and Tricycle Agent, Millhams Street and Church Street, Christchurch".[105] Possibly one of the reasons for this move was to provide capital for the new line introduced in September, the 'Salvo-Quadricycle', a four-wheeled machine later acquired by Queen Victoria (after which it became known as the 'Royal Salvo'). Clarke was "Sole Agent for the District" and for six months invited the public to "Call and See the most wonderful Machine of the day" which he claimed was "Not for an Age, but for All Time". It was a claim which, with the wisdom of hindsight, we can see was slightly exaggerated.

From March 1879, Ernest Clarke advertised two additional lines having little to do with cycles—sewing machines and insurance (he was agent for the British Equitable Assurance Company). The picture changes again later in the year, when he entered into partnership with his fellow-member of the bicycle club, James Lawrence. An imposing display, depicting the 'Flying DutchmanBall-bearing Tricycle', advertises the new firm of Clarke and Lawrence from November 1879 until the end of the following year. There is also an advertisement running for four weeks for "a respectable youth" to assist the partnership.[106] Six months later another advert seeks "a sharp boy".[107] Obviously these were busy times—or maybe the "respectable youth" was not quite sharp enough.

At the beginning of 1880 the new partnership moved into the High Street premises adjoining the Ship Hotel (as it then was), formerly occupied by the presumably now defunct fusee-chain business. The firm's letterhead shows premises that, to the biased eye of the veteran-cycle enthusiast, present a much livelier and more attractive sight than any modern car showroom. Although cycles predominate, an even more diverse range of goods was now being sold, from perambulators to horse-clippers. Not forgetting skates, when the moment seemed propitious.

From the beginning of 1881 a different advertisement showed that the partnership now had premises in Lymington (St. Thomas Street) as well as Christchurch. But this is quickly altered in February, when the short-lived venture with James Lawrence ends with Ernest Clarke buying him out for just under £300.[108] We do not know what went wrong. But Lawrence is not recorded as a member of the bicycle club after this date, and Ernest continues on his own at both the Christchurch and Lymington addresses.

For the next few years things appear to proceed quietly at the shops. The Christchurch business cannot have been helped by the decline in the cycling activities of the club. Doubtless to help promote business, Clarke organised a draw for a 'Flying Dutchman' tricycle, valued at fifteen guineas. It is unlikely the venture was entirely successful, since an advert "about 40 tickets left at 2s. each" is repeated verbatim five weeks running.[109]

But the standard of living enjoyed by the family cannot have been too low, for on two occasions we find Mrs. Clarke advertising for a "general servant".[110] And in the summer of 1882 Ernest sailed his fifteen-foot boat *Lady Godiva* (the Coventry connection again!) in a series of matches on Thursday afternoons, being placed third overall at the finish of the competition,[111] as well as sailing in the Mudeford Regatta.[112] He was later secretary of the Christchurch Sailing Club.[113] A few months pass and another interest is disclosed: "Mr. Ernest Clarke's St. Bernard bitch 'Nun' was highly commended on Tuesday last, at the Crystal Palace Dog Show" (she had previously won first prize at the Birmingham National Dog Show).[114] We also know that Clarke was secretary and treasurer of the local amateur fire brigade at this time.[115] Cycles were clearly now more a way of earning a living than a way of life.

The advertising for the business, which had been running for years in the local press, finally stopped in October 1885. All, sadly, became clear the following month:

A Local Bankruptcy Case. The first meeting of creditors in the case of Edward Ernest Clarke, cycle agent and grain merchant, Christchurch, was held at the Criterion Hotel, Bournemouth, on Wednesday, Mr. F. Aston Dawes, official receiver, presiding.[116]

The "grain merchant" activities had almost certainly been subsidiary to the cycle business, and indeed the largest trade creditors by quite a long way were the cycle manufacturers Messrs. Starley & Sutton, of Coventry, who were owed £143 10s. 8d. This was the firm responsible for the proceedings, and they obviously felt little sympathy for Clarke's plight. "In reply to a question as to whether he had any offer to make, the debtor said he could not get the security necessary for an offer; and further Messrs. Starley & Sutton, who had forced him into bankruptcy, had declared that they would accept no composition, but would make him bankrupt, adding that anything they could do to make it hot for him he might depend upon their doing. In these circumstances, he thought it would be useless to make an offer."

Ernest Clarke's principal creditor was in fact his father, William Clarke, of Coventry, to whom he owed £360. After Starley &

Sutton, the next in size were Messrs. Ferrey & Co., of Christchurch, £53 9s. 2d.—Ernest's father-in-law's firm (possibly another loan, as they were drapers). The brewers Devenish & Co., of Weymouth, were next at £51 11s. 6d. (presumably to do with the grain merchant side of the business), then Messrs. Rudge & Co., cycle manufacturers of London at £22 1s. 0d., followed by a number of smaller local and other creditors. We are told the debtor's statement disclosed total liabilities amounting to £1,098 16s. 1½d., while the assets were estimated to produce a gross total of only £426 2s. 0d.

Mr. Clarke "gave as the cause of his insolvency bad debts, depression in trade, heavy rent, and depression in the value of stock. His annual personal and household expenditure had been about £200". Apart from the Coventry firm, everyone seems to have been sorry to be involved in the downfall of this lively and likeable Christchurch character. "The Official Receiver, in the course of the proceedings, said the books kept by the debtor were about the best kept books he had seen since he first commenced under the new Act" (the Bankruptcy Act, 1883). "He must also candidly say further that he had heard nothing whatever against Mr. Clarke." Several of the creditors present also expressed their regret that a composition could not be arranged, but at the end of the proceedings the debtor was adjudicated bankrupt and a trustee appointed.

Nothing more is heard of "Ernest Clarke, cycle agent". Yet it appears a family tradition had been started, for in the early years of the 20th century we find *Kelly's Directory* listing "Ernest James Clarke, cycle maker, 3, Castle Street, Christchurch". It seems Ernest's son was carrying on where his father had left off.

8. Persecution and prosecution

IT IS well-known that the path of the early bicyclists and tricyclists was a stony one in more ways than one. A general public used for centuries to pedestrians and horse traffic only on the roads, did not take too kindly to the velocipede or bicycle. Christchurch was no exception. A resident complains to the local newspaper:

> Sir, I appeal to your columns for redress against 'bicycles without bells'. Ought not every bicycle to carry a bell, or something to warn passengers, whether on foot, on horse back, or in a carriage, that they are coming. In some places every bicycle is compelled to carry a bell. Hoping that something may yet be done,
> I remain, yours sincerely, E. F. Maberly.
> Avonmouth House, Christchurch, Hants.[117]

This brought a swift response from the young bicycle club:

> Sir, having seen a letter in your paper of last week's impression relating to bicycle bells, we beg to state, that in the rules of the Christchurch Bicycle Club, all members are particularly requested to have a bell attached to their machines.
> We would wish to call your numerous readers' attention to the fact that on the evening of the 16th inst., some malicious person or persons placed a row of bricks across the road at Burton, well knowing the club would be returning that way from Sopley, and which might have been attended with most serious consequences, had not a pedestrian fortunately discovered and removed them. We have offered a reward of 20s. to any person who shall give such information as will lead to the conviction of the offenders.
> We are, sir, yours obediently,
> Ernest Clarke (Captain),
> C. W. Bollard (Hon. Sec.).[118]

The implication is clear. In the eyes of the club, they were more sinned against than sinning. This may well be true, and certainly it was the Mayor's view at the 1880 dinner, but it was not the only grouse. Another correspondent writes:

> Sir, I beg leave to ask through you if any law exists in relation to the use of bicycles in our towns allowing the occupation of the street in parallel lines or restricting them when more than one to following as nearly as may be the line of the foremost. About to cross a narrow part of the street and near an angle three came up nearly parallel with each other, and to my great danger had not a loud whistle by one of the riders reached me just in time.
> An Old Inhabitant. Christchurch, May 2nd, 1878.[119]

The rebuttal this time is even more immediate, and is by the newspaper itself following a report on a run in the same issue:

Although we are not of those who say that bicycles ought to be put down or taxed, we think our correspondent today has a right to be heard in his complaint that bicycle riders sometimes ride "all of a heap", but these must be strangers, for we believe the regulations of the Christchurch Bicycle Club insist upon its members riding single file. [120]

Occasionally the exchange became more heated. The *Christchurch Times* of 14 September 1878 contains a lengthy report of a summons for assault brought by Frank Davis (possibly a relative of A. H. Davis of the bicycle club) against Edward Newcomen, dealt with in the local magistrates court. Davis claimed that Newcomen (a pedestrian) had deliberately pushed him off his 52 in. wheel 'Excelsior' bicycle, so that he fell against one of the two Christchurch town bridges and badly injured himself. Newcomen cross-summoned on the basis that Davis had subsequently assaulted him. After deliberating for some minutes, the magistrates dismissed both cases, taking the view there was insufficient evidence to convict.

Harassment was not only carried out by the general public. The police were swift to prosecute for any infringement of the county byelaws regulating the use of bicycles, made under the Highways and Locomotives Amendment Act, 1878. Before this date cyclists had been less restricted in their activities, hence the complaints. During the late 1870s and early '80s (and no doubt subsequently) there are a number of reports of prosecutions, usually for riding a bicycle between sunset and sunrise without a lamp, or riding on the footpath, the common penalty being a fine and the payment of costs totalling together ten or fifteen shillings. A standard excuse, in the former case, was that the defendant's oil lamp had gone out unnoticed during the journey. There were few if any local prosecutions for "furious riding", which in the metropolis frequently attracted the maximum penalty of forty shillings. There is no recorded instance of a prosecution of any member of the Christchurch Bicycle Club.

Local cyclists were not always on the receiving end when it came to proceedings in the magistrates court. A leading bicyclist in the area, at the time a member of the Christchurch club, was prepared to take action to enforce the wheelman's rights as a user of the highway:

The toll keeper at Lytchett Gate, near Bournemouth, who has recently refused to open her gate to bicyclists, having been officially complained of by Mr. H. Carr Gibbs, of the Christchurch B.C., was ordered by the Clerk of the Turnpike Trust to open the gate for the future. She, however, still declines, and Mr. Gibbs, who is a Consul

*of the B.T.C., and a member of the B.U., has very properly taken
out a summons against her. We shall be very glad to hear the result,
and to publish it.*

This was an editorial comment in *The Cyclist* for 6 April 1881.
Just a week later we find a full report under the heading "Important
Prosecution—a Toll-gate Keeper Convicted". After considerable
legal argument (the facts being largely undisputed) the chairman of
the magistrates "said the bench were clearly of opinion that the
gate should have been opened, and the defendant must pay the
nominal fine of one penny and costs".[121] No doubt the cyclist
left the court well-satisfied.

 POOLE.—Formed Aug.
1878 ; 38 mem.; capt., J. W.
Hansford ; uniform, grey,
with polo cap of same, and
brown stockings ; badge,
arms of the town of Poole,
with wreath of oak leaves
worked on cloth in gold and
silver lace ; en. fee , 5s.;
sub. 5s.; hon. sec., J. W. White, Seldown,
Poole ; hdqts. London Hotel, Poole.—
Grand meet and opening of (gravel) racing
track, July 14th, 1880 ; also sports, racing,
&c. Track 4 laps to the mile, 18 feet
wide. Racing colours, green and black.
President, Lord Wimborne.

RINGWOOD.—Formed March, 1879;
25 mem.; capt,, W. Ghoimes; uniform,
dark green : badge, monogram ; no en. fee;
sub., 2s. 6d.; hon. sec., Bernard Jones,
High-street, Ringwood; hdqts., Seldown
House, Ringwood.—Annual meet held
August 26, 1880; number present, 70.

 BOURNEMOUTH. —
Formed Oct., 1877 ; 110
mem. ; capt., Fred.
J. Oliver; uniform, dark
brown ; badge, silver
monogram : no en. fee ;
sub. 10s. : hon. sec.,
Fred. A. K. Hounsell ;
hdqts., Gervis Arcade.
Bournemouth.—Annual race meeting held
on Whit-Mondays.

 WANDERING MIN-
STRELS. — Formed June,
1879 ; 15 mem.; capt., Mor-
timer Oldham Heath; uni-
form, black polo cap, black
coat,shepherd's plaid knicks.,
black stockings, and black
and white tie ; badge, a shield;
en. fee, 2s. 6d. ; sub.. 2s. 6d. ;
hon. sec., Clement John Haydon, Ebford
House, Wimborne Minster, Dorsetshire ;
hdqts., Tapper's Railway Hotel.

ABOVE: montage of local clubs (from 'Icycles', a Christmas 1880
bicycle annual). The formation dates support Christchurch's claim
to be "the oldest club down here".

OPPOSITE: the Flying Dutchman continued for some time to be the principal
attraction in Ernest Clarke's shop.

ERNEST CLARKE,

BICYCLE,

TRICYCLE,

SEWING MACHINE,

AND

GENERAL AGENTS,

HIGH STREET AND

MILLHAMS STREET,

CHRISTCHURCH.

A couple on the aptly-named Sociable Tricycle, photographed at Lyndhurst. The post on the right would have pointed to Beaulieu, seven miles away, and the site of a future generation's National Motor Museum. The date is most likely the early 1880s.

9. Mudeford Bicycle Club

"TO BICYCLISTS!!! To meet a pressing want a few gentlemen contemplate establishing a Bicycle Club at Mudeford. Gentlemen wishing to join may, on a production of a certificate as to their sanity, and also an undoubted proof of their respectability, obtain full particulars of the Hon. Sec. (pro. tem.), Club Room, Mudeford. —No quill drivers or counter jumpers will be eligible".[122] The date was May, 1879. It would appear the object of the exercise was to form an elitist organisation as an alternative to the more cosmopolitan club already established a couple of miles away in the centre of Christchurch. "Quill drivers" and "counter jumpers" probably referred to clerks and shop assistants. Certainly the advertisement could be expected to attract the mildly eccentric. According to one of the national cycling periodicals, it was "inserted by a 'pilled' candidate".[123] The following week it appeared in more sober form: "Mudeford & District Bicycle Club. Gentlemen desirous of joining should apply to the Hon. Sec. Mr. J. Grunsell, Carriage Manufacturer and Bicycle Agent, Purewell, Christchurch".[124]

Whichever advert brought the replies, the new Christchurch club got off to a strong enough start. We read of a meeting on 12th June:

Mudeford and District Bicycle Club. At a meeting held in the Club room on Thursday evening, Mr. G. Grossmith in the chair, sixteen members were enrolled, the various officers were elected and a committee appointed. It was also decided to furnish the room with a bagatelle board, chess, draughts and other games, and to provide various newspapers and periodicals.[125]

This was obviously the inaugural meeting. Another week passes and we have:

A first general meeting of the members of the Mudeford Bicycle Club and Institute was held on Thursday evening, when several new members were proposed. It now numbers twenty members. The code of rules as prepared by a committee was adopted, and the necessary officers and committee were elected.[126]

At a committee meeting held afterwards, the decision to supply the reading room with papers and games was confirmed.

The first reported event was the club's attendance at the highly successful meet of the Christchurch Bicycle Club on 10 July 1879. It will be recalled that the new club mustered five riders, under the leadership of Captain Last, having already equipped themselves with a uniform which was "very natty". Clearly there was no real antagonism between the two Christchurch clubs, or they would not have been invited to the meet. We read also that "several members" (of the Mudeford club) "mustered at their headquarters at Stanpit, on Thursday evening, and left to attend a bicycle meet at Ringwood".[127] Six members of the Christchurch club also attended, the event being briefly reported at the beginning of September 1879:

A meet of the members of several of the neighbouring clubs took place on Thursday week, under the auspices of the Ringwood club. The head quarters were at the White Hart Hotel, from whence a short run was amde. About 50 riders were present.[128]

But on the whole the new club maintained a low profile, being absent from other meets at this period, and no runs being recorded. The Mudeford club (referred to as the Mudeford Cricket & Bicycle Club) were indirectly involved later in the year in a prosecution under the licensing laws. They had taken a room at Nelson Cottage, Mudeford (said to be the site of the present Nelson Inn), above an off-licence. The licensee was charged with allowing persons to consume beer *on* his premises. A police officer said:

He went to the defendant's house at Mudeford on the 12th September, between 8 and 9 p.m. He went to a room upstairs where he found eleven persons, drinking beer, and some were playing cards, and others playing chess. He drunk some of the beer and took the names of the persons present . . .[129]

After evidence had been given that the large upstairs club-room was blocked off from the premises below, the only means of access being a fixed ladder, the magistrates dismissed the case.

The 1880 season started on 22 April with the joint run to Lymington, eight members of the Mudeford club attending. Next month they were present at the first Bournemouth Whitsun meet. Two months later, on 24 June, they were represented at the second annual Christchurch meet. And this is really all we know of the Mudeford Bicycle Club, otherwise the Mudeford & District Bicycle Club, otherwise the Mudeford Cricket & Bicycle Club.

By way of a footnote, further reference should perhaps be made to J. Grunsell, the Mudeford club's honorary secretary. From the date the organisation started for exactly a year he advertised regularly in the *Christchurch Times:* "For all kinds of Bicycles and Tricycles apply to James Grunsell, Coach Builder, Christchurch, and Secretary to the Mudeford Bicycle Club. Repairs neatly executed. The Best and Cheapest Machines in the trade."

The competition can hardly have endeared him to the Captain of the Christchurch club. The advert omits the reference to the secretaryship from mid-January 1880, and adds a mention of "New and Second-hand Dog Carts and Phaetons" from the end of March.

From June 1880, at least so far as the pages of the *Christchurch Times* are concerned, Ernest Clarke (at this stage with his partner James Lawrence) again becomes the town's sole dealer. James Grunsell remained in business in Purewell for several years, but it seems his main trade was as a coach builder and not a cycle agent.

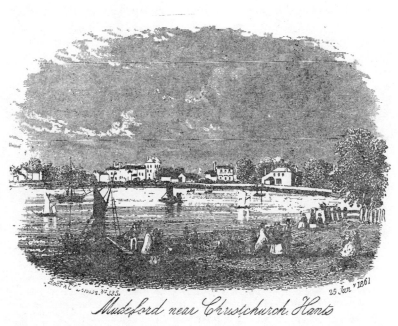

Mudeford near Christchurch Hants

Victorian Mudeford—"a small watering-place on the edge of Christchurch Bay"

10. The Dual Tricycle

WE HAVE spoken of a link between fusee-chain manufacturing and the cycle trade at the beginning of the chapter on Ernest Clarke. By an odd coincidence we find another Christchurch tie-up between the two trades in another part of the town a few years later:

> We have the satisfaction of noting that Mr. Jeans, of the old watch-chain firm of Jenkins and Co., has set about establishing in our midst what to us seems to bid fair to be a thriving industry, and although at present the 'hands' employed may be counted upon the fingers, yet we do not at all despair in seeing before long, large numbers employed upon the manufacture of the 'Dual Tricycle'.[130]

Williams Jeans' invention is shown at the end of the chapter. In essence, it employed a patented arrangement, using intermediate wheels operated by levers, whereby the machine could be driven by either of the big 48 in. wheels, the gearing being different in each case so that the wheel on one side was high-geared for level runs, the other being low-geared for hills. Although early in the tricycle era, this was not the first variable-gear machine produced—the 'Omnicycle' tricycle had been fitted with a somewhat similar device in 1879.

A local photograph roughly contemporary with Jeans' tricycle shows that the general design, as opposed to the gearing, was not unique. Both tandem tricycles (where the couple sat one behind the other) and 'sociables' (where as here they sat side by side) were common at this stage.

Jeans gave his machine a stiff trial run before it came on the market. *The Cyclist* for 19 October 1881 tells the story:

> In the Storm. Mr. William Jeans, who has patented and is bringing out a new speed and power gearing for tricycles, set out on Thursday for Bournemouth, from Coventry, in order thoroughly to test his invention, and such was his enthusiasm that he faced the gale of Friday as a pretty good test of a foul weather machine. He says "I ran from Banbury to Oxford in a little under five hours, which is not so bad considering I had every now and then to heave the branches of trees out of the way, and I just escaped getting the bulk of an elm tree across my precious frame."

Initially the appropriately-named 'Dual Tricycle' was manufactured by the Zephyr Bicycle & Tricycle Co. of Coventry, under an arrangement with the inventor. It was exhibited on their stand at the Stanley Show (the nineteenth century cyclist's equivalent of today's motor show) in February 1882. It was described in an exhibition supplement of *The Cyclist*: "Another novelty. Jeans' patent

'Dual' tricycle, with power wheels on one side and speed gear on the other, either usable at will by a very ingenious arrangement of intermediate wheel gear. It is likely to become very popular in time".

The *Tricyclists Indispensable Annual*, 1882 shared the view that "this is a well-made strong machine . . . it runs well, and is a good, useful article". After the first batch of machines had been manufactured and found to be "esteemed favourites by tricycle riders",[131] William Jeans set about constructing them himself at the Jenkins & Co. factory in Christchurch. This was apparently still owned by the Jenkins family, though run by Mr. Jeans and a Mr. Rose.[132] From October, 1882, the *Christchurch Times* carries a regular advert for the new invention.

The invitation to purchase only continued until the end of January 1883. Possibly the inventor ran into some sort of difficulty, financial or otherwise. Maybe he sold out to a larger concern. There is no reference to the 'Dual' in *Bicycles and Tricycles of the Year* 1886, a pretty comprehensive catalogue of the items then extant. But there is a brief reference to a 'Hill-climbing Zephyr', and it could be that Jeans eventually disposed of his patent to the company which had first manufactured his machine. *Kelly's Directory for Hampshire* for 1885 lists 'Jenkins & Co., watch fusee chain manufacturers, Bridge Street, Christchurch', and according to Allen White[133] the factory did not finally close until 1914. Contrary to the situation in the High Street, the cycle did not at these works replace the fusee chain.

The Dual Tricycle. William Jeans's 1882 tricycle was manufactured in Christchurch. Its six gearingwheels appear complicated but apparently worked well.

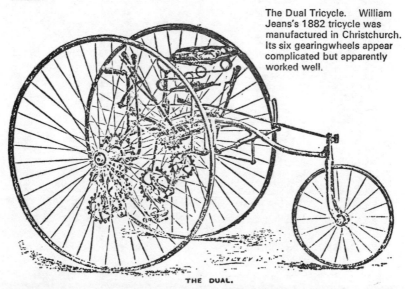

THE DUAL.

11. Calendar of events

APPENDIX 1.   CALENDAR OF RECORDED EVENTS

Date	Event	References***	
6 July 1876	Inaugural meeting—4 mem.	BN 29.3.78	BA 1878
12 July 1876	Sopley run—5 mem.	BN 29.3.78	
2 April 1877	Salisbury run—17 mem.+	BO 7.4.77	
31 May 1877	Lymington run—9 mem.+	BO 2.6.77	
15 June 1877	Frampton v. Phillips race	CT 23.6.77	
27 Sept. 1877	Bournemouth run—14 mem.	BN 5.10.77	
27 Sept. 1877	General meeting	BN 5.10.77	
11 Oct. 1877	General meeting	BN 5.10.77	BO 20.10.77
15 Oct. 1877	General meeting—new rules	BN 19.10.77	BO 20.10.77
22 Oct. 1877	Sopley run	BN 19.10.77	
26 Dec. 1877	Paper chase—10 mem.	CT 29.12.77	BO 29.12.77
16 Jan. 1878	Sopley run—bricks on road	BO 23.1.78	
Jan. 1878	Newtown run	BO 23.1.78	
Jan. 1878	Cranemoor run	BO 23.1.78	
31 Jan. 1878	Crichel run—19 mem.	BO 2.2.78 CT 2.2.78	BJ 1.2.78
13 Mar. 1878	Sopley run—12 mem.	BO 16.3.78	
18 Mar. 1878	Ringwood run	BN 29.3.78	
19 Mar. 1878	First annual dinner—25m.+	BO 23.3.78	CT 23.3.78 BN 29.3.78
25 Mar. 1878	A.G.M.	BO 30.3.78	
April 1878	London tour—2 mem.	CT 4.5.78	
2 May 1878	Lymington run—25 mem.	CT 4.5.78 BN 10.5.78	BO 4.5.78 BJ 8.5.78
9 May 1878	Wimborne run—12 mem.	CT 11.5.78	BO 11.5.78 BN 17.5.78
23 May 1878	Paper chase—15 mem.	BN 31.5.78	
30 May 1878	Informal racing—17 mem.	BN 7.6.78	BO 8.6.78
10 June 1878	Southampton meet—9 mem.	BT 20.6.78	BN 21.6.78
10 June 1878	Bournemouth races—4 mem.	BT 20.6.78	CT 15.6.78
20 June 1878	Bournemouth run—20 mem.	BN 28.6.78	BT 27.6.78
2 July 1878	Committee meeting	BT 11.7.78	
15 July 1878	Sopley moonlight run—9 mem.	BN 26.7.78	BT 25.7.78
16 July 1878	Bransgore run	BT 11.7.78	
17 July 1878	Newtown run	BT 11.7.78	
18 July 1878	Poole run	BT 11.7.78	
July 1878	Cranemoor run	BT 11.7.78	
1 Aug. 1878	Cricket match v. Sports Club	CT 3.8.78	
29 Aug. 1878	Hordle run—Shakers— 16 mem.	BN 6.9.78	
5 Sept. 1878	Ringwood run—7 mem.	BN 13.9.78	BT 12.9.78
10 Sept. 1878	Sopley m/l run—13 mem.	BN 20.9.78	BT 19.9.78
11 Sept. 1878	Ringwood m/l run—11 mem.	BN 20.9.78	BT 19.9.78
12 Sept. 1878	Lymington m/l run—9 mem.	BN 20.9.78	BT 19.9.78
26 Sept. 1878	Bournemouth run to see race	BT 3.10.78	C Nov., '78
26 Sept. 1878	Jenkins v. Boxall race	BT 3.10.78	C Nov., '78
26 Sept. 1878	General & committee meetings	BT 3.10.78	C Nov., '78
3 Oct. 1878	Sports Club dinner—27 mem.	C Nov., 78	BO 5.10.78
11 Oct. 1878	Sopley m/l run—7 mem.	C Nov., 78	BN 18.10.78 BT 17.10.78
15 Oct. 1878	Committee meeting	C Nov., 78	BN 25.10.78 BT 24.10.78
17 Oct. 1878	Bournemouth races (Jenkins)	C Nov., 78	BT 31.10.78 BO 19.10.78
5 Nov. 1878	Fireworks display	BT 14.11.78	BN 15.11.78

Date	Event		
		CT 9.11.78	BO 9.11.78
7 Nov. 1878	Sopley m/l run—11 mem.	BT 14.11.78	BT 31.10.78
		BN 15.11.78	C Nov., '78
8 Nov. 1878	Newtown m/l run	BT 31.10.78	C Nov., '78
11 Nov. 1878	Ringwood m/l run—2 mem.	BT 14.11.78	BT 31.10.78
		BN 15.11.78	C Nov., '78
12 Nov. 1878	Bournemouth m/l run	BT 31.10.78	C Nov., '78
13 Nov. 1878	Bransgore m/l run	BT 31.10.78	C Nov., '78
14 Nov. 1878	Sopley m/l run	BT 31.10.78	
21 Nov. 1878	Concert in Town Hall	BN 29.11.78	C Jan., '79
		BO 23.11.78	CT 23.11.78
4 Dec. 1878	Sopley m/l run—4 mem.	BN 13.12.78	C Jan., '79
5 Dec. 1878	Bournemouth m/l run—lecture	BN 13.12.78	C Jan., '79
6 Dec. 1878	Bransgore m/l run	BN 13.12.78	C Jan., '79
9 Dec. 1878	Ringwood m/l run—2 mem.	C Jan., 79	
6 Jan. 1879	Sopley run	BT 23.1.79	C Jan., '79
7 Jan. 1879	Newtown run	BT 23.1.79	C Jan., '79
8 Jan. 1879	Kinson run	BT 23.1.79	C Jan., '79
9 Jan. 1879	Milton run	BT 23.1.79	C Jan., '79
10 Jan. 1879	Hinton run	BT 23.1.79	C Jan., '79
4 Feb. 1879	Sopley run	BT 27.2.79	BN 28.2.79
4 Feb. 1879	Committee meeting	C Feb., 79	
5 Feb. 1879	Newtown run	BT 27.2.79	BN 28.2.79
6 Feb. 1879	Milton run	BT 27.2.79	BN 7.3.79
7 Feb. 1879	Bournemouth run	BT 27.2.79	BN 7.3.79
25 Feb. 1879	Committee meeting	C Feb., 79	
			C May, '79
19 Mar. 1879	Second annual dinner	BN 4.4.79	BO 22.3.79
		CT 22.3.79	BT 27.3.79
25 Mar. 1879	A.G.M.	C May, 79	CT 29.3.79
			BT 3.4.79
April 1879	Easter tour London/Brighton	BN 11.4.79	BN 25.4.79
		C May, 79	BT 10.4.79
April 1879	Ringwood & Bournemouth run	BN 11.4.79	BN 25.4.79
		C May, 79	BT 10.4.79
April 1879	Bournemouth races (Jenkins)	BN 11.4.79	BN 25.4.79
		C May, 79	BT 10.4.79
1 May 1879	Ringwood run	BT 1.5.79	C Jun, '79
2 May 1879	Newtown run—3 mem.	BT 1.5.79	BT 15.5.79
			C June, '79
5 May 1879	Cranemoor run—7 mem.	BT 1.5.79	BT 15.5.79
			C June, '79
7 May 1879	Sopley run	BT 1.5.79	C June, '79
8 May 1879	Lymington run—16 mem.+	CT 10.5.79	C June, '79
		BO 10.5.79	BN 16.5.79
		BT 1.5.79	BT 15.5.79
14 May 1879	Cox v. Howlett race	CT 17.5.79	
15 May 1879	Wimborne meet—9 mem.	C June, 79	BT 1.5.79
			CT 17.5.79
22 May 1879	Ringwood meet—10 mem.	C June, 79	BT 29.5.79
		BT 1.5.79	CT 24.5.79
		BO 24.5.79	BN 30.5.79
29 May 1879	Bournemouth run—10 mem.	C June, 79	BT 1.5.79
		BT 5.6.79	BO 31.5.79
			BN 6.6.79
2 June 1879	Bournemouth races (Frampton)	BT 12.6.79	BO 7.6.79
2 June 1879	Christchurch meet/photograph	BO 31.5.79	BT 13.6.79
		BO 7.6.79	CT 7.6.79
12 June 1879	Ringwood meet—18 mem.	BT 19.6.79	BN 20.6.79
		BO 14.6.79	CT 14.6.79
19 June 1879	Poole meet—19 mem.	BN 26.6.79	BN 3.7.79
		BT 26.6.79	BO 21.6.79

24 June 1879	Special general meeting	CT 5.7.79	BT 19.6.79
26 June 1879	Bournemouth sports—5 mem.	BN 4.7.79	BT 3.7.79
10 July 1879	Christchurch meet—30 mem.	C Aug., 79	CT 5.7.79
		CT 12.7.79	BN 18.7.79
		BT 17.7.79	BO 12.7.79
24 July 1879	Bournemouth meet—13 mem.	CT 26.7.79	BT 31.7.79
		BN 1.8.79	
25 July 1879	Crewkerne races (Jenkins)	CT 26.7.79	
31 July 1879	Blandford meet—7 mem.	CT 2.8.79	BO 2.8.79
4 Aug. 1879	Chichester races (Jenkins)	CT 9.8.79	
14 Aug. 1879	Poole meet—8 mem.	BT 21.8.79	BT 18.9.79
			BN 22.8.79
19 Aug. 1879	Yeovil races (Jenkins)	CT 23.8.79	
28 Aug. 1879	Ringwood meet—6 mem.	BT 4.9 79	BN 5.9.79
			CT 6.9.79
4 Sept. 1879	Bournemouth run—7 mem.	BN 12.9.79	BT 11.9.79
18 Sept. 1879	Taunton races (Jenkins)	CT 29.9.79	
2 Oct. 1879	Sports Club dinner	BO 4.10.79	
28 Oct. 1879	Sopley m/l run—7 mem.	BT 16.10.79	BT 6.11.79
29 Oct. 1879	Cranemoor m/l run	BT 16.10.79	
30 Oct. 1879	Bournemouth m/l run—5 mem.	BT 16.10.79	BT 6.11.79
5 Nov. 1879	Annual Fireworks display	BT 13.11.79	CT 8.11.79
25 Nov. 1879	Sopley run—3 mem.	BT 4.12.79	
10 Feb. 1880	Third annual dinner—30/40 m.	TC 25.2.80	C Mar., '80
		BO 14.2.80	BN 20.2.80
		CT 14.2.80	BT 19.2.80
24 March 1880	A.G.M.	BN 26.3.80	BN 9.4.80
			BT 25.3.80
22 April 1880	Lymington run—12 mem. +MBC	BT 29.4.80	BN 30.4.80
			BT 6.5.80
8 May 1880	Lillie Bridge races (Jenkins)	WYB 1881	
17 May 1880	Bournemouth meet/races— 15 mem.	BT 27.5.80	BN 28.5.80
		TC 26.5.80	C June, '80
20 May 1880	Wimborne run—6 mem.	BN 28.5.80	BT 27.5.80
22 May 1880	Stamford Bridge races (Jenkins)	WYB 1881	CT 29.5.80
24 June 1880	Annual Christchurch meet	BT 1.7.80	TC 7.7.80
		CT 26.6.80	BN 2.7.80
			WW Aug., 80
5 July 1880	Retirement dinner, C. W. Bollard	TC 14.7.80	
26 Aug. 1880	Ringwood meet	CT 28.8.80	
5 Nov. 1880	Annual fireworks display	BO 13.11.80	CT 13.11.80
29 Mar. 1881	A.G.M.—resolve join B.U.	C May, 1881	WW May '81,
		BN 8.4.81	BT 7.4.81
12 May 1881	Wimborne run—2 mem.	BT 19.5.81	BN 20.5.81
8 Sept. 1881	Annual Christchurch meet	BO 10.9.81	
13 Oct. 1881	Bicycle Union meeting London	BT 20.10.81	BU mins.
23 Feb. 1882	New billiard table received	BO 25.2.82	
10 April 1882	Taunton races (Jenkins)	TC 19.4.82	
6 May 1882	Southampton races (Jenkins)	WWA 1883	TC 10.5.82
29 May 1882	Bournemouth races (Jenkins)	CT 3.6.82	TC 7.6.82
29 Mar. 1883	A.G.M.—20 mem.	BO 31.3.83	
April 1883	Invited to Bournemouth meet	BO 28.4.83	
Nov.–Dec. 1883	Billiard handicap @ clubroom	BO 3.11.83	BO 8.12.83
7 May 1884	Special general meeting— change of name & new rules	BO 10.5.84	

***For reference abbreviations see "Text references", page 57.

BICYCLE RIDING.

J.W. WHITE.

1. The good old days had their own old ways Of ri . ding, and seem to have been contented Though they could not sing of Bi . cy . cling for the sim . ple rea . son it wasn't in . ven . ted If they'd tried it they might not have made it... suc . ceed So we

2. To spin a . long a good le . vel road With the breeze at your back If there's wind at all No hill in sight, no horse to take fright No fear of a spill, no thought of a fall No gates to pay on the broad high . way Not a

12. Recorded members

1876/77
E. E. Clarke C

1877/78
F. Bemister
C. W. Bollard S
W. E. Burt SC *
E. E. Clarke C
F. Cox *
J. B. Frampton
G. Gossling
E. W. Jenkins *
W. Lane
A. S. Reakes
A. Street
W. Street SC
F. Whitcher
Sir H. D. Woolf P

1878/79
J. Bentley *
C. W. Bollard S
V. Bradley
A. Brown
W. E. Burt SC
E. E. Clarke C
J. B. Frampton
G. Gossling
Green
Hall
Hicks
E. W. Jenkins
J. Lawrence
J. Lockett*
G. Moore*
Oakley
C. Payn
A. S. Reakes
F. Reeks
W. Reeks
F. Scaife *
A. Street
W. Street
J. Topham *
Turner
J. W. White
Sir H. D. Woolf P

1879/80
F. Bemister
C. W. Bollard S & T
W. E. Burt *
E. E. Clarke C
F. Cox
A. H. Davis
J. B. Frampton
G. Gossling
T. Gossling
E. W. Jenkins
F. A. Lane *
J. Lawrence *
W. A. Marshall
C. Payn
H. Payn
W. J. Payn
W. Reeks
A. J. Salter
W. C. Sparkes *
A. Street
W. Street SC
R. Wheal
J. W. White
Sir H. D. Woolf P

1880/81
C. W. Bollard S
W. E. Burt* S
E. E. Clarke C
R. Druitt *
G. H. Ferrey
E. W. Jenkins
J. A. M. Lamas +
H. Lane
J. Lawrence T
W. A. Marshall *
Rev. Z. Nash VP
C. Reeks
W. Street SC
G. K. B. Tighe +
H. Willedge
J. W. White *
Sir H. D. Woolf P

1881/82
W. E. Burt*
E. E. Clarke C+
H. C. Gibbs+
J. B. Jenkins +
E. W. Jenkins
F. A. Lane *
J. H. Leney *
W. A. Marshall +
Rev. Z. Nash VP
H. Perkins T
W. C. Sparkes S
A. Street *
W. Street SC
J. W. White *
Sir H. D. Woolf P

1882/83
C. E. B-Young VP
E. E. Clarke C+
H. Davey, M.P. VP
G. Ferrey, jun. T
E. W. Jenkins SC
Rev. Z. Nash VP
W. C. Sparkes S
Sir H. D. Woolf P

1883/84
C. E. B-Young VP
E. E. Clarke C+
H. Davey, M.P. VP
G. Ferrey, jun. T
E. W. Jenkins SC
J. B. Jenkins +
Rev. Z Nash VP
H. Reeks
W. C. Sparkes S
Sir H. D. Woolf P

Abbreviations:—
C — Captain
SC — Sub-Captain
S — Secretary
T — Treasurer
P — President
VP — Vice-President
* — Committee member
+ — Member of Bicyclists Touring Club

Membership note: The club started with 4 members and rose to "about a score" by October 1877. Most of the members during the late 1870s are recorded. The membership roughly doubles to "nearly 60" at February 1880, and continues at this sort of level thereafter, but principally only the names of officers and committee are known.

Dedicated to the

Christchurch Bicycle Club

BICYCLE RIDING

SONG

Words and Music
BY
J. W. WHITE.

Ent. Sta. Hall.

Price 3/-

London:
ALFRED PHILLIPS, KILBURN ROAD. N. W.

13. Club songs

Bicycle Riding: the club song, composed by J. W. White for the March, 1878, dinner and published by Alfred Phillips of London shortly afterwards is reproduced facing pages 52 and 53, with its front cover being shown opposite.

The Captain's Song: words adapted by J. W. White from Gilbert & Sullivan's 'H.M.S. Pinafore' for the March, 1879, dinner:-

Captain —	I am the Captain of the C.B.C.,
Club Chorus —	And a right good captain too;
Captain —	You are very, very good, and be it understood,
	I command a good club too.
Club Chorus —	We are very, very good, etc.

Captain —	Though racing's not my style,
	I keep on mile after mile;
	However bad the roads may be,
	I'm never known to quail and come back home by rail,
	And I never get a spill you see.
Club Chorus —	What, never?
Captain —	No, never,
Club —	What, never?
Captain —	Well, hardly ever
	I hardly ever get a spill you see.
Club Chorus —	So give three cheers, with three times three,
	For the jolly Captain of the C.B.C.

Captain —	I do my best to satisfy you all
Club —	And with you we are quite content;
Captain —	You are exceedingly polite, and I think it only right
	To return the compliment.
Club —	We're exceedingly polite, etc.

Captain —	Bad language or abuse I never, never use,
	Whatever the emergency;
	Though "bother it" I may
	occasionally say,
	I never use a big, big D.
Club Chorus —	What, never?
Captain —	No, never,
Chorus —	What, never?
Captain —	Hardly ever
	Hardly ever swear a big, big D.
Chorus —	So give three cheers and three times three, etc.

Captain —	So here's good luck to the C.B.C.,
Club —	And good luck to its Captain too;
Captain —	And may twice as many men,
	When next we meet again,
	Be found with us members new.
Club Chorus —	And may twice, etc.
Captain —	We're the oldest club down here,
	And I think we need not fear
	However many new we see,
	And at every fixed club run
	I hope that every one
	Will never from us absent be.
Club —	What never?
Captain —	Hardly ever from us absent be.
Club —	Then give three cheers and three times three, etc.

"The C.B.C.": composed by J. W. White and sung at the February, 1880, dinner. The lyric and verses unknown, but the chorus as follows:—

> "Oh, we're jolly good fellows in the C.B.C.,
> We're very jolly fellows, so we all agree,
> For we all love one another,
> And our captain as our brother,
> We're so awfully united in the C.B.C."

Note: J. W. White was not the only club composer. We know that in 1878 Ernest Clarke himself composed and sung "a very humerous song". Unfortunately, the words and lyric are unrecorded.

14. Text references

BA	—	"Bicycle Annual"
BJ	—	"The Bicycle Journal"
BN	—	"Bicycling News"
BO	—	"Bournemouth Observer & Christchurch Chronicle"
BT	—	"The Bicycling Times"
BU mins.	—	Bicycle Union minutes
C	—	"Cycling"
CT	—	"Christchurch Times"
TC	—	"The Cyclist"
WW	—	"Wheel World"
WWA	—	"Wheel World Annual"
WYB	—	"Wheelman's Year Book"

Ch. 1.
1. BJ 20.10.76
2. BO 22.3.79
3. BN 29.3.78
4. CT 11.8.77
5. BO 7.4.77
6. BO 2.6.77
7. CT 23.6.77
8. BN 5.10.77
9. BN 25.2.76
10. CT 29.12.77
11. BN 5.10.77
    BN 19.10.77
    BO 20.10.77
12. CT 26.1.78 CT 4.5.78
13. BO 12.1.78
14. White's Directory for Hampshire, 1878
15. BN 29.3.78
16. BO 2.2.78
17. C Dec., 79
18. C Dec., 79

Ch. 2.
19. CT 4.5.78
20. BN 10.5.78
    BN 26.3.80
    BT 25.3.80
22. BT 7.6.77
23. BN 31.5.78
24. BN 7.6.78
25. BT 20.6.78
26. CT 15.6.78
27. BO 17.10.77
28. CT advert 16.11.78
29. BO 22.3.79
30. BN 26.7.78
31. CT 3.8.78
32. BN 6.9.78
33. BT 3.10.78
34. BT 3.10.78

Ch. 3.
35. C Nov., '78
36. BN 25.10.78

Ch. 4.

37. BN 13.12.78
38. BN 13.12.78
39. CT 2.11.78
40. CT 9.11.78
41. BN 15.11.78
42. BO 2.11.78
43. BN 29.11.78
44. C May, 79
45. CT 22.3.79
46. BO 22.3.79
47. CT 29.3.79
48. BO 10.5.79
49. CT 29.3.79
50. BN 25.4.79
51. BO 10.5.79
52. BO 10.5.79
53. CT 17.5.79
54. CT 17.5.79
55. CT 24.5.79
56. BT 29.5.79
57. CT 7.6.79
58. BO 7.6.79
59. CT 14.6.79
60. BN 3.7.79
61. CT 5.7.79
62. BT 25.3.80
    BN 26.3.80
63. BN 4.7.79
64. CT 12.7.79
65. BO 12.7.79
66. BT 18.9.79
67. CT 2.8.79
68. BO 4.10.79
69. CT 8.11.79
70. BO 14.2.80
71. BO 14.2.80
72. BO 14.2.80
73. BN 9.4.80

Ch. 5.
74. BN 30.4.80
    BT 29.4.80
75. BN 28.5.80
76. BO 22.5.80
77. WYB 1881
78. BN 28.5.80
79. CT 26.6.80
80. TC 14.7.80
81. CT 28.8.80
82. CT 28.8.80
83 BO 30.10.80
84. BO 13.11.80
85. BN 8.4.81 BT 7.4.81
86. BT 20.10.81 BU mins.
87. BT 19.5.81
88. BO 10.9.81
89. CT 3.10.81
90. BO 25.2.82

Ch. 6.
91. TC 7.6.82
92. BO 31.3.83
93. BO 28.4.83
94. CT 19.5.83
95. BO 3.11.83
96. BO 8.12.83
97. CT 12.4.84
98. BO 10.5.84
99. Kelly's Directory of Hampshire.
100. TC 25.2.80 Wiltshire and Dorsetshire, 1899 and 1903 editions.

Ch. 7.
101. CT 21.10.76
102. London Gazette 6.9.77
103. CT 6.1.77
104. CT 7.9.78
105. CT advert 6.7.78–31.8.78
106. CT 15.11.79–6.12.79
107. CT 19.6.80
108. BO 7.11.85
109. CT 14.1.82–11.2.82
110. CT 28.5.81 CT 1.7.82
111. BO 14.10.82
112. BO 16.9.82

113. Kelly's Directory, 1885
114. BO 20.1.83
115. Tucker's Christchurch Almanack, 1883
116. BO 7.11.85

Ch. 8.
117. CT 19.1.78
118. CT 26.1.78
119. CT 4.5.78
120. CT 4.5.78
121. TC 13.4.81
122. CT 31.5.79
123. BT 12.6.79
124. CT 7.6.79
125. CT 14.6.79
126. CT 21.6.79
127. CT 30.8.79
128. CT 6.9.79
129. CT 4.10.79

Ch. 9
130. CT 13.5.82
131. CT 13.5.82
132. "The Chain Makers", p.22, Allen White
133. "The Chain Makers", p.22, Allen White

Ch. 10.

Index

Aldridge, C. 36
Alington, Lord 8
'Ashley Arnewood' (House) 11
Assault summons by bicyclist 43
Bath Hotel, Bournemouth 6
Bell Inn, Hordle 15
Bemister, S. (Mayor) 17, 26
Bicycle clubs, growth of 4, 5, 36, 37
Bicycle Touring Club (now C.T.C.) 9, 44
Bicycle Union (now B.C.F.) 32, 44
Blandford 25
Blandford B.C. 24, 25, 30
Bollard, C. W. 6, 7, 8, 18, 19, 22, 26, 27, 30, 31, 32, 42
Boscombe 6, 7, 21
Bournemouth 6, 13, 15, 17, 23, 24, 25, 29, 30, 35
Bournemouth Bicycle Club 13, 22, 24, 25, 30, 31, 33
Bournemouth Grosvenor B.C. 30, 31
Bournemouth Yeomanry Cavalry, race with C.B.C. 5
Boxall, R. 15, 29, 30
Bradley, V. 17
Bransgore 6, 17
Brighton 21
Burt, William Eaton 11, 19, 20, 30, 32
Burton 5, 14
Carr-Gibbs, H. 43, 44
Cat and Fiddle Inn, Hinton 6
Christchurch Bicycle Club: annual dinners 9, 17, 19, 26
billiards/billiard tables 20, 26, 27, 34, 36
bricks in path of 42
bugles/bugle calls 11, 12, 14, 15, 33
change of name to Twynham Club 35
club-room/headquarters 7, 8, 16, 19, 20, 21, 26, 31, 33
concert 18, 19
cricket match v. Sports Club 14
cups/awards 17, 20, 27, 33
firework displays 18, 26, 32, 33
formation 4
general meetings 10, 16, 20, 24, 27, 32, 35, 36
machines used by 21, 22
meets attended 12, 22, 23, 24, 25, 29, 30, 31, 33, 35, 46
members, number of 4, 5, 7, 9, 10, 17, 19, 21, 26, 27, 35
paperchases 7, 12
racing at Bournemouth 13, 15, 23, 24, 29, 30, 35
racing track proposed 13, 19, 27
rules/subscription 7, 16, 17, 24, 36, 42, 43
runs 4, 5, 6, 7, 8, 9, 11, 12, 14, 15, 17, 19, 21, 26, 27, 29, 30, 31, 32, 33, 35
skating activities 26
songs 10, 14, 19, 20, 27
tours 19, 21
uniform 11, 26
Christchurch Cycling Society 36
Clark, Edward Ernest 4, 5, 6, 7, 8, 9, 10, 11, 13, 14, 17, 18, 19, 20, 22, 25, 26, 27, 33, 35, 36, 38, 41 (marriage, business and other activities, bankruptcy) 42
Cortis (Champion) 30
Cox, F. 21
Crichel House, near Wimborne 8
Crown, The, Ringwood 22
Crown, The, Wimborne 8
Davey, Horace, M.P. 9
Downton 5
Dual Tricycle (invention and early marketing of) 48, 49
Ferrey, George (Mayor) 13, 15, 19, 27, 38
Fordingbridge 5
Frampton, James B 6, 7, 12, 13, 23, 24
Fusee-chain manufacturing 38, 39, 48, 49
Gossling, G. 7
Grossmith, G. 45
Grunsell, J. 45, 46, 47
Hansford (Poole Captain) 21, 24, 29
Heathpoult (Inn), Bournemouth 6
Hordle 15
Howlett, A. 21
Jeans, William (Inventor of 'Dual Tricycle'), 48, 49
Jenkins, E. Walter 6, 7, 12, 13, 14, 15, 19, 20, 23, 24, 25, 26, 29, 30, 35, 36
Kings Arms, Christchurch 19, 23, 25, 26, 30
Lane, F. A. 37
Lansdowne Hotel, Bournemouth 6
Last (Mudeford Captain) 25, 45
Lawrence, James 4, 39
London Hotel, Bournemouth 29
Lymington 6, 11, 21, 29, 39
Lymington B.C. 24, 25, 31
Marshall, W. A. 27
Matthews (Host) 9
Mead, Dr. H. T. H. 17
Milton (New Milton) 11, 15
Mudeford Bicycle Club 24, 25, 29, 30, 45–47 (history)
Nash, Rev. Zachary 28
Newlyn, N. S. 19, 23, 25
Newtown (Highcliffe) 15
Non-local bicycle clubs: Chichester,

12, 30, Saturn 21, Basingstoke, Brixton Ramblers, Castle Wanderers, (Sturminster Newton), Clapham, Fareham, Isle of Wight, Pickwick, Portsmouth, Shaftesbury, South Hants, Winchester, 29
Pain, H. (Mayor) 20, 27
Parkstone B.C. 33
Phillips, Fred 6
Pokesdown 6, 7
Poole 5, 24, 25
Poole Bicycle Club 22, 24, 25, 29, 33
Prince and Princess of Wales 8
Prosecutions of early cyclists 43
Railway, use of 8, 9, 21, 26
Reakes, A. S. 19
Reekes, Herbert 36
Reeks, W. 22
Ringwood 9, 22, 24, 25, 31, 46
Ringwood Bicycle Club 22, 23, 24, 25, 29, 30, 31, 33, 46
Roads, condition of 5, 17, 26, 30, 33
Rose, James and Henry 8
Salisbury 5
Salvation Army 24
Shakers (Evangelical group) 15
Ship, The, Christchurch 9
Sopley 4, 5, 14
Southampton 12
Southampton B.C. 12, 29
Sparkes, W. C. 32, 33, 36

Stanley, H. M. 17
Stanley Show, The 48
Street, W. 7, 8, 22
Temperance Hotel, Christchurch 7
10th Hants Rifle Volunteers Band 25, 26, 30, 32
Toll-gate, right of bicyclists to use 43, 44
Town Hall, Ringwood 31
Tricycle riding 21, 24, 25, 31, 33, 38, 39, 40, 48, 49
Wandering Minstrels B.C. (Wimborne) 29, 30, 31
White Hart Hotel, Ringwood 46
White, J. W. 10, 19, 27
Williams, Rev. J. L. 25
Wimborne 8, 12, 22, 30, 32
Wimborne Minster B.C. 24, 25, 30, 33
Winkton 14
Woolf, Sir Henry Drummond, M.P. 9, 10, 13
Wool Pack, Sopley 14

This index covers the ten chapters of the book. Reference should also be made to the Calendar of recorded events, Analysis of recorded membership and club songs. The illustrations have also not been indexed

60